# HOW TO THINK LIKE
# CHURCHILL

By the same author:

*How to Think Like Sherlock*
*How to Think Like Steve Jobs*
*How to Think Like Mandela*
*How to Think Like Einstein*

# HOW TO THINK LIKE
# CHURCHILL

## DANIEL SMITH

Michael O'Mara Books Limited

For Dad

This paperback edition first published in 2023
First published in Great Britain in 2015 by
Michael O'Mara Books Limited
9 Lion Yard
Tremadoc Road
London SW4 7NQ

A CIP catalogue record for this book is available from the British Library.

Papers used by Michael O'Mara Books Limited are natural,
recyclable products made from wood grown in sustainable forests.
The manufacturing processes conform to the environmental
regulations of the country of origin.

ISBN: 978-1-78929-596-2 in paperback print format
ISBN: 978-1-78243-331-6 in e-book format

1 2 3 4 5 6 7 8 9 10

Designed and typeset by Envy Design Ltd

Printed and bound by CPI Group (UK) Ltd, Croydon, CR0 4YY

www.mombooks.com

# Contents

# Introduction

'In the great drama, he was the greatest of all.'

GENERAL CHARLES DE GAULLE, WRITING TO
QUEEN ELIZABETH II ON CHURCHILL'S
DEATH IN 1965

When Winston Churchill was born on 30 November 1874 into one of the great English aristocratic families, it might have seemed like he was destined to leave his mark on the world. In fact, his path to greatness was by no means smooth. Brought up by parents who always kept their distance, his childhood was tainted by unhappiness. He emerged from school marked out as one who 'could do better' and opted to join the military, since his academic achievements would not guarantee him an elite university place.

Driven by a combination of brazen ambition, some sense of entitlement, his own deep-seated demons and, let it be said, a genuine sense of duty, he launched a twin career as army man and journalist. Within a few years he had made himself independently rich and extraordinarily famous throughout the Empire. He was now ready to embark on his journey of public service, entering the House of Commons in 1900.

His would prove to be a remarkable political career, in which he changed party twice – from the Conservatives to the Liberals and back again. For a while he was something of a young radical, pushing through ground-breaking social reforms. At other times he displayed a distinctly conservative bent, winning notoriety (at least retrospectively) for his distrust of the Suffragette movement, for his ruthless actions during the 1926 General Strike and for his distinctly politically incorrect attitudes towards empire. Neither friend nor enemy was ever entirely sure of what to expect from Winston.

After he was caught up in arguably the biggest military disaster to befall the Allies in the First World War – the ill-fated Gallipoli expedition – his chances of continuing a first-rate political career seemed to be over. He spent large parts of the next quarter-century sidelined to a greater or lesser extent. In the 1930s he was both ridiculed and reviled by rivals who accused him of war-mongering as they pursued a policy of appeasement towards Hitler. Of course, history would find very much in Churchill's favour.

In 1940, aged sixty-five, he could look back on a distinguished career, full of ups and downs. Had he packed up then for the quiet life back at his beloved Kent home at Chartwell, he would have been remembered as one of the giants of early twentieth-century British life. As it was, he became prime minister of a coalition government (an arrangement that always seemed to suit his temperament better than one-party governments) and led Britain from her darkest hour to her finest one. By fending off the Nazi menace when it seemed destined to overrun Europe, he bought the world the time and space needed to ultimately defeat Hitler's armies. In doing so, he won for himself the reputation as the greatest Briton who ever lived.

The attributes he displayed between 1940 and 1945 included the ability to galvanize a population suffering intense hardships and daily threats to life and limb. Through some of the finest oratory ever heard and by sheer force of will, he dragged the nation through the war while partners in Europe were collapsing. Refusing to ever countenance defeat or surrender, he saw British forces negotiate many delicate rearguard actions until, from around 1943, they were able to get onto the front foot once again. That he kept his nerve and, by hook or by crook, made so many strategic 'right calls' helped turn imminent defeat into ultimate victory.

By the time the war was over, he was seventy, and utterly entitled to enjoy the quieter life. Instead, he unsuccessfully fought that year's general election. Despite the Labour Party's victory stinging him badly (could anyone, after all, have given more to the country in those previous five years?), he remained a public figure beloved like no one else. But just six years later he was back in the top job. Now he used his diminishing energies to counter the threat of Cold War oblivion, seeking an accommodation with the Soviets and striving to establish a special relationship with the US. Half American by birth, and with the ability to see that America had been gradually superseding Britain as the dominant Western power, it was a relationship he had pursued fervently for decades.

Time inevitably took its toll, but he left public life only in 1964 when he gave up his backbench seat. He died on 24 January 1965, a little after his ninetieth birthday, and was accorded a full state funeral, the only civilian to be given such an honour in the twentieth century.

For a man who had so many distinct phases to his life, it is hard to pin down exactly who the real Winston Churchill was. In the popular imagination, he is the bulldog-like figure who smoked fat cigars, buoyed the public with his speeches and threw victory signs to the waiting press pack during the war. Indeed, this may have been him at his finest. But there were a great many more sides to his personality – little lost boy, uncompromising man of empire, social reformer, soldier, peace-lover, journalist, Nobel laureate, politician, painter, bricklayer, connoisseur of the good life, optimist, depressive, flawed family man and father of the nation.

In the half-century since he died, there can be no contemporary British figure whose story has been so scrutinized as Churchill's. Of course, he has his critics, and sometimes with good reason. He could be stubborn and impetuous, driven by ego and sometimes unsympathetic to the plight of others (especially if they were not British, English-speaking or from a 'Christian civilization'). The morality of a few of his actions – such as giving permission for the blanket bombing of German cities – continues to divide opinion sharply. But few credibly argue that he was anything other than a giant figure of his age and one who, for all his faults, delivered what the British nation needed at its most acute time of crisis. By historical quirk, Hitlerism gave Churchill the opportunity to cast himself as a hero, and he seized his moment with courage and charisma.

*How to Think Like Churchill* looks at the personality traits, ideas, beliefs and some of the other key influences that informed his actions at the various stages of his life and helped define his world view. As with the other subjects in the series, there emerges a figure who is nothing if not complex, combining extraordinary strengths and attributes with humbling weaknesses.

# Landmarks in a Remarkable Life

1874     Winston Leonard Spencer-Churchill is born at Blenheim Palace in Oxfordshire on 30 November to Rt. Hon. Lord Randolph Churchill (the third son of the 7th Duke of Marlborough) and his American wife, Jennie Jerome.

1880     Winston's brother, John Strange Spencer-Churchill, born on 4 February.

1882     Winston attends St George's School in Ascot, Berkshire.

1884     Moves from school in Ascot to one in Hove.

1888     Begins at Harrow School.

1893     Commences training as a cavalry cadet at Sandhurst Royal Military Academy.

1895     Winston's father dies on 24 January, aged forty-five. Winston joins the 4th Hussars as a second lieutenant and is granted permission to serve with the Spanish forces in Cuba, coming under live fire for the first time. He also makes his first visit to the USA.

1896    Posted with the army to India.

1897    Serves with the Malakand Field Force on the North-West Frontier.

1898    Is present at the Battle of Omdurman in Sudan.

1899    Retires from the army to pursue his political ambitions. Fails to win the parliamentary seat for Oldham in Lancashire. Travels to South Africa as a journalist, reporting on his experiences. He is briefly held as a prisoner of war by the Boers before making an audacious escape. Afterwards joins the South African Light Horse.

1900    Elected Conservative Member of Parliament (MP) for Oldham. Publishes first and only novel, *Savrola*.

1901    Makes maiden speech in Parliament. Joins the Territorial Army and is later commissioned as a captain in the Queen's Own Oxfordshire Hussars.

1904    Swaps allegiance from the Conservative Party to the Liberal Party.

1905    Appointed Under-Secretary of State for the Colonies.

1906    Elected Liberal MP for the Manchester North West constituency.

1907     Becomes a Privy Councillor.

1908     Becomes Liberal MP for Dundee in Scotland, a seat he holds until 1922. He completes a landmark year by marrying Clementine (Clemmie) Hozier on 12 September and being appointed President of the Board of Trade.

1909     The Churchills' first child, Diana, is born.

1910     Becomes Home Secretary in February, holding the post for some eighteen months.

1911     A son, Randolph, is born. Churchill appears on the scene at the infamous Siege of Sidney Street. In October he is named First Lord of the Admiralty.

1914     Outbreak of First World War. Churchill personally oversees the defence of Antwerp for a period in October. Meanwhile, Clemmie gives birth to a second daughter, Sarah.

1915     Resigns as First Lord of the Admiralty in May following the Dardanelles disaster. Becomes Chancellor of the Duchy of Lancaster, a post he holds until November. He also rejoins the army and sees active service on the Western Front in the First World War.

1917     Appointed Minister of Munitions in the wartime coalition of David Lloyd George in July.

1918     End of First World War. A third daughter, Marigold, is born.

1919  Named Secretary of State for War and Air.

1921  Appointed Secretary of State for the Colonies, a post he holds until October 1922. He also plays a key role in the negotiation of the Irish Treaty. His mother dies in June and Marigold, his youngest daughter, is killed by septicaemia in August.

1922  Loses parliamentary seat in election in Dundee. Clemmie gives birth to a fourth daughter, Mary. The Churchills purchase Chartwell Manor in Kent, which becomes a beloved refuge.

1923  Fails to win parliamentary by-election in West Leicester. The first volume of his history *The World Crisis* appears. The fifth and final volume appears in 1931, completing Churchill's analysis of the years 1911-28.

1924  Fails to win parliamentary by-election in the Abbey Division of Westminster but in October becomes 'Constitutionalist' MP for Epping in Essex, serving the constituency until 1945. Defects back to the Conservatives, becoming Chancellor of the Exchequer in November.

1925  Returns Britain to the Gold Standard.

1926  Comes out as a determined opponent of the General Strike.

1929  Resigns as Chancellor after Labour's victory in the June general election.

1930s    Churchill's 'wilderness years', during which time he does not hold high office and is a peripheral figure within Parliament. He is, though, outspoken in his warnings of the growing threat from Hitler's Germany and becomes a staunch opponent of the government's policy of appeasement. He also uses the decade to write, make international lecture tours and pursue his interest in painting.

1930    Publishes the autobiographical *My Early Life*.

1933    Hitler becomes Chancellor of Germany. Churchill publishes first volume of *Marlborough: His Life and Times* (the fourth and final volume appeared in 1938).

1938    Churchill leads condemnation of the Munich Agreement agreed by Neville Chamberlain that cedes the Sudetenland from Czechoslovakia to Germany.

1939    Outbreak of the Second World War. Britain declares war on Germany in September following the Nazi invasion of Poland. Churchill is once again drafted in as First Lord of the Admiralty.

1940    Replaces Neville Chamberlain as prime minister in May at the head of a wartime coalition. Bolsters the nation as it contends with the Blitz, the Battle of Britain and the Dunkirk evacuations.

| | |
|---|---|
| 1941 | Russia and the USA enter the War and Britain declares war on Japan. |
| 1942 | Churchill approves the blanket bombing of selected German cities. General Montgomery leads the Allied forces to victory at the Battle of El Alamein in North Africa, an event Churchill describes as potentially the 'end of the beginning' of the war. |
| 1943 | The Allies push German forces out of North Africa and invade Italy. Churchill attends the Tehran Conference, the first conference to include each of the 'Big Three' Allied leaders – Churchill, Roosevelt and Stalin. |
| 1944 | The Russians break the Germans' siege of Leningrad after some 872 days. D-Day sees Allied troops land on the Normandy coast of France in May, paving the way for the end of German occupation, first in France and then throughout western Europe. |
| 1945 | End of the Second World War as first Victory in Europe is secured and then, after the use of two atomic bombs, Japan is defeated. Churchill attends the Yalta and Potsdam conferences alongside Stalin and, firstly, President Roosevelt (at Yalta, in February) and then President Truman (at Potsdam, in July) to establish Europe's post-war reorganization. He briefly heads a Conservative caretaker government following the dissolution |

of the wartime coalition. However, the Conservatives are defeated by Clement Attlee's Labour Party at the general election in July. Churchill becomes Conservative MP for Woodford in Essex, the constituency he serves until retiring from the House of Commons in 1964.

1946    In a speech delivered at Fulton College in the USA, Churchill warns of the 'Iron Curtain' descending across Europe.

1948    Publishes *The Gathering Storm*, the first volume of six in his epic history of the Second World War. The last volume appears in 1953.

1951    Leads the Conservatives to general election victory and begins a second term as prime minister.

1952    Mau Mau Uprising in Kenya begins.

1953    Receives the Nobel Prize for Literature and is made a Knight of the Garter.

1955    Resigns as prime minster on 5 April owing to failing health.

1956    Publishes the first volume of the four-volume *History of the English-Speaking Peoples*.

1963    Becomes an honorary citizen of the United States. His daughter, Diana, commits suicide in October.

1964    Retires as a parliamentarian in July.

1965    Dies in London on 24 January, aged ninety. He is given a state funeral and is buried, in accordance with his wishes, in St Martin's churchyard in Bladon, Oxfordshire.

# Don't Let a Slow Start Hold You Back

'I was what grown-up people in their offhand
way call a "troublesome boy".'

WINSTON CHURCHILL IN *MY EARLY LIFE*
(PUBLISHED 1930)

Winston Leonard Spencer-Churchill was born in Blenheim Palace, a resplendent stately home in the Oxfordshire countryside of England, on 30 November 1874. It is difficult to think of a more spectacular location from where to make your grand entry into the world.

He was descended from John Churchill, the First Duke of Marlborough and one of the great military figures of the late-seventeenth and early eighteenth centuries. Doubtless the Duke's finest moment was the victory he masterminded in 1704 on German soil at the Battle of Blenheim, during the War of the Spanish Succession. His triumph having won him glory and financial riches back in England, Marlborough set about building the magnificent family home that he would name after the battle.

Winston's father, Lord Randolph Churchill, was himself a major public figure. He was elected MP for the Woodstock constituency in Oxfordshire the same year as Winston was born, and so began a rapid rise up the greasy political pole that saw him widely tipped as a prime minister-in-waiting by the 1880s. In 1886 he took another step in that direction when the incumbent prime minister, Lord Salisbury, named Churchill as Chancellor of the Exchequer. Randolph certainly had the ambition to make a tilt for the top job, but in the end it was his lust for advancement that arguably caused his downfall. Allowing himself to get into a metaphorical arm-wrestle with Salisbury that he could not win, his career went into something of a tailspin and Churchill would die in 1894 – while only in his mid-forties – embittered and marginalized.

Winston was by then emerging from a childhood that did little to suggest he would come anywhere near to matching the achievements of his illustrious predecessors. He was prone to ill-health, had various speech impediments (including a lisp and a stammer) and boasted an academic record that could at best be described as patchy. His school report from 1888, for instance, detailed several of his faults including forgetfulness, carelessness and a lack of punctuality.

He began his schooling at St George's in Ascot aged eight, and his various physical frailties made him an obvious target for bullies. It was, perhaps, this experience that made him so determined to stand up to apparently mighty foes in later life. Regardless, his time at St George's was a deeply unhappy one in which he received brutal treatment from fellow students and staff alike. As a result, he left to move to a much less prestigious establishment (although one he enjoyed a great deal more) – the Misses Thompson Preparatory School in Hove, near Brighton, on England's south coast. Then, in 1888, he began four years at Harrow, one of the great public schools of England (and alma mater of no less than eight British prime ministers).

It is often said that Churchill was an academic slouch, but that is to overstate the case at least a little. True, he was no great mathematician, a weakness that at one stage threatened his entry into the Royal Military College at Sandhurst until he finally did just enough to pass in 1893. However, he had a decent grasp of literature and geography, was not the worst at French and was very strong in history (even if to the modern eye he was somewhat uncritical in his absorption of the dominant imperial narratives of the age). He had extra-curricular success too, becoming the public schools' fencing champion.

However, school just did not really suit him. His parents and those who taught him marked his card early as a lazy under-achiever. His grandmother was only a little more generous, once observing: 'He is a clever boy and really not naughty but he wants a firm hand.' Yet his schoolmasters were unable to get the best out of the young Winston. In *My Early Life*, his 1930 autobiographical work, he would describe his school days as '… not only the least agreeable, but the only barren and unhappy period of my life.' His woe was compounded by what we would probably now consider to be a dysfunctional relationship with his parents. To read the correspondence between them from his school days is quite heart-rending, with Winston constantly seeking their approval and their consistent refusal to grant it.

Winston idolized his father well into adulthood, as exemplified by the highly (and probably unjustly) complimentary biography he would write of him in 1905. Randolph was a spectre throughout much of Winston's life and the son mirrored the father in certain respects. For instance, they both suffered forms of depression, both had great oratorical skills, both were fiercely ambitious and both prone to episodes of bad judgement. Yet father and son never came to know each other well on a personal level, with Randolph prioritizing his career to the virtual exclusion of his offspring.

Perversely, he almost seemed to wield power over his son through rejection. For example, as Winston struggled to navigate his post-Harrow path (it took him three attempts to get into Sandhurst), Randolph warned him that he seemed destined for a 'shabby, unhappy and futile existence'. The barbs, though, did not lessen Winston's esteem for his father. As he put it in an article for the *Strand Magazine* in February 1931: 'Although I had talked with him so seldom and never for a moment on equal terms, I conceived an intense admiration and affection for him and, after his early death, for his memory.'

In contrast, Churchill's mother Jennie had a much deeper bond with Winston. Nonetheless, she too could be distant. The daughter of a wealthy New York businessman, she died in 1921, having had to cope for many years as a widow – a situation not aided by

Randolph leaving her with considerable debts. But she was also a product of her class and age, and thus kept up a barrier between herself and her son. As he recalled in *My Early Life*: 'I loved her dearly – but at a distance.' In fact, arguably the closest relationship of Winston's childhood was with his beloved nanny, Mrs Everest. 'She had been,' he would write, 'my dearest and most intimate friend during the whole of the twenty years I had lived …'

Churchill may have seemed, literally, to the manor born, but his childhood was a challenging one, marked by loneliness, underachievement and disappointment. Few who saw him at twenty would have guessed at the great things that lay ahead. For all the knockbacks, though, Churchill himself had deep reserves of self-belief that would quickly propel him into the national consciousness. But whether even he believed he would eclipse his eminent ancestors so comprehensively is doubtful.

# Address Your Shortcomings

'I have no technical and no university education,
and have just had to pick up a few things
as I went along.'
WINSTON CHURCHILL, 1949

If the school system had failed to bring out the best in Churchill he made sure to further himself once he was out of its clutches. He was, in certain respects, one of history's great autodidacts. Many of the subjects he loathed when forced upon him as a student, he came to love (or at least respect) in later years.

Take the speech he made at the University of Oslo in 1948, in which he admitted that he had changed his views regarding the study of classical literature. He had a strong dislike for the subject at school, failing 'to respond to the many pressing and sometimes painful exhortations which I received to understand the full charm and precision of the classic languages'. Now, as a senior statesman, he recognized the role of the classics as what he called a 'unifying influence' in Europe and the wider modern world.

None of which is to say that Churchill looked back on his relative lack of success at school with particular regret. Indeed, he was convinced that his experiences played their part for better and worse in moulding him as an adult. For one thing, he came to believe that his mastery of the English language was, in part at least, the result of his exclusion from the realms of the 'cleverer boys'. That he was placed in the lowest class gave him an 'immense advantage' over his ostensibly brighter contemporaries, he would argue, because while they were sent off to study Latin and Greek, he was left to focus on his native tongue. He described the situation thus in *My Early Life*:

> We were considered such dunces that we could learn only English. Mr. Somervell – a delightful man, to whom my debt is great – was charged with the duty of teaching the stupidest boys the most disregarded thing – namely, to write mere English … Thus I got into my bones the essential structure of the ordinary British sentence – which is a noble thing.

He went on to say how when in later years his peers, celebrated for their skill with Latin and Greek, had to re-engage with English, he felt himself at no disadvantage.

Having eventually secured his place at Sandhurst, Churchill began to blossom. He was from the outset a skilled horseman and he graduated eighth out of an intake of some 150 young men, subsequently signing up with the 4th Hussars cavalry regiment in February 1895. Sandhurst also provided him with an opportunity for academic self-improvement, a chance he seized eagerly by reading extensively – mostly works supplied by his mother. In spare moments he devoured novels, histories, philosophy and economic treatises.

Ever the pragmatist, and as a leading figure of a small island nation that in his own lifetime could still call itself the world's greatest power – taking in a fifth of the global population under the aegis of its empire at its peak – Churchill came to appreciate the role of innovation and enterprise in the country's success. He was not blind to the economic benefits inherent in a well-functioning education system. 'Those who think we can become richer or more stable as a country by stinting education and crippling the instruction of our young people,' he warned in a speech at a school in 1925, 'are a most benighted class of human beings.' It was a topic he returned to even amid the intensity of the Second World War, when the country's immediate survival was his principal concern. In a wireless broadcast in 1943, he declared, 'The future of the world is to the highly educated races who alone can handle the scientific apparatus necessary for pre-eminence in peace or survival in war.'

But, ultimately, he believed in a liberal education in its truest sense – one geared toward developing the person as a whole. In 1948 he gave a speech at the University of London in which he expanded upon the subject: 'The first duty of the university is to teach wisdom, not a trade; character, not technicalities,' he said. It is a pretty close approximation of the education he provided for himself in his post-school years. Having on his own initiative filled many of the gaps left by school, it was what he was happy to describe as 'a curious education'.

Underpinning his self-teaching was his desire for

deep engagement with history, for what is history if not a collection of stories shedding light on what lies behind both success and failure? His determination to learn lessons from history came through time and again in his utterances. Addressing the House of Commons in 1936, for instance, he said, 'We cannot undo the past, but we are bound to pass it in review in order to draw from it such lessons as may be applicable to the future …' Eight years later, when he was prime minister, he told a meeting of the Royal College of Physicians: 'The longer you look back, the farther you can look forward.' And in 1953 he told James Humes – an up-and-coming speech-writer for Eisenhower who would go on to craft words for three more presidents, Nixon, Ford and Reagan – 'Study history, study history – in history lie all the secrets of state craft.'

Churchill's greatness as a wartime leader cannot be put down to any single cause, but his sound grasp of history – encompassing everything from military strategy to the personality traits of leaders both good and bad – informed his decision-making, his leadership style and even his oratory, especially in his first tenure as prime minister. That he was subsequently recognized by the Nobel awarding committee as a world-leading historian in his own right was the final, wonderful riposte to all those schoolmasters (and indeed his own father) who sincerely doubted that he would ever amount to much.

## READ LIKE CHURCHILL

'Young people, I believe, should be careful in their reading, as old people in eating their food. They should not eat too much. They should chew it well.'

**WINSTON CHURCHILL IN AN ESSAY, 1934**

Churchill was a voracious reader known for his ability to process vast quantities of text and to quickly grasp its key points. Here is an extremely abridged list of titles and authors that hints at the eclectic nature of his reading:

- *Annual Register: A Record of World Events.* A vital reference work published annually since 1758 that Churchill began reading while still a small boy. It proved a trusty source of knowledge on current affairs upon which he often relied throughout his life.
- Aristotle (384–322 BC). Polymath student of Plato and arguably the first great scientist in history.
- Charles Darwin (1809–82). English naturalist who formulated theories of evolution and natural selection in *On the Origin of Species* and *The Voyage of the Beagle*.
- Edward Gibbon (1737–94). British historian whose most significant work is *The History of the Decline and Fall of the Roman Empire*. 'I devoured Gibbon,' Churchill said. 'I rode triumphantly through it from end to end and enjoyed it all.'
- Henry Hallam (1777–1859). Historian whose

*Constitutional History of England* was particularly influential on Churchill.

• Rudyard Kipling (1865-1936). Poet and storyteller for children and adults who emerged as the pre-eminent chronicler of the British Empire, winning the Nobel Prize for Literature in 1907. Key works include *The Jungle Book, Just So Stories, Puck of Pook's Hill* and *Kim*.

• T. E. Lawrence (1888-1935). Also known as Lawrence of Arabia, he and Churchill became close friends, with Lawrence spending a spell in the 1920s acting as Churchill's advisor in the Colonial Office. *Seven Pillars of Wisdom*, Lawrence's autobiographical account of his involvement in the 1916-18 Arab Revolt, was published in 1922 and has been cited as Churchill's favourite book.

• William E. H. Lecky (1838-1903). Irish historian who wrote extensively on religion, rationalism and ethics. He also authored the well-received *History of England During the Eighteenth Century*.

• Lord Macaulay (1800-59). A leading Whig politician of the age and author of a famous and influential *History of England*. Churchill had learned by heart another of his works, *Lays of Ancient Rome*, while at school, but came to regard him as 'the prince of literary rogues, who always preferred the tale to the truth …', largely because of Macaulay's unsympathetic take on the First Duke of Marlborough.

• Thomas Malthus (1766-1834). British cleric and

political economist whose key work, *An Essay on the Principle of Population*, argued that human population would always be curbed by the likes of war, famine, illness and natural disaster.

- W. Somerset Maugham (1874–1965). Author and playwright who reached superstar status with works including *Liza of Lambeth*, *Of Human Bondage* and *The Moon and Sixpence*. Maugham and Churchill would become friends.
- Plato (428/7–348/7 BC). One of the great figures of Greek philosophy and learning.
- Winwood Reade (1838–75). Historian, philosopher and adventurer whose influence on Churchill is discussed in more detail in the chapter 'Come to an Accommodation with God'.
- Arthur Schopenhauer (1788–1860). Philosopher behind *The World as Will and Representation*.
- Sir Walter Scott (1771–1832). Great Scottish historical novelist whose books such as *Ivanhoe*, *Rob Roy* and *Waverley* no doubt appealed to Churchill's taste for adventure.
- Adam Smith (1723–90). His 1776 work *An Enquiry into the Nature and Causes of the Wealth of Nations* served as the basis of the modern academic discipline of economics.
- Robert Louis Stevenson (1850–94). Another Scottish storyteller who specialized in tales of adventure like *Treasure Island* and *Kidnapped*.

## Address Your Shortcomings

We also know from bookseller inventories that the Churchill bookshelves included collected volumes of, among others, Jane Austen, the Brontës, Lord Byron, Thomas Carlyle, Miguel de Cervantes, Thomas De Quincey, John Dryden, George Eliot, Henry Fielding, William Hogarth, Dr Johnson, John Locke, John Milton, Molière, Plutarch, Edgar Allan Poe, Jean Racine and William Wordsworth.

For a man who is quoted in the English language perhaps more than anybody, with the exception of Shakespeare, it is interesting to note that Churchill was a great fan of quotation collections too. They were, he found, a short cut to unending pools of knowledge.

'It is a good thing for an uneducated man to read books of quotations … The quotations when engraved upon the memory give you good thoughts.'

WINSTON CHURCHILL IN *MY EARLY LIFE*, 1930

# Entertain Ambition

'It is better to be making the news than taking it;
to be an actor rather than a critic'

WINSTON CHURCHILL IN *THE STORY OF
THE MALAKAND FIELD FORCE*, 1897

Even as others doubted his potential as a young man, there is little evidence to suggest that Churchill ever let setbacks unduly knock his confidence. He seems to have maintained a belief that he would make a name for himself even in the face of the grimmest adversity. Ironically, he derived much of his self-confidence and unbridled ambition from the father who did so much to undermine the young Winston.

Some of Churchill Jr's self-belief no doubt stemmed from a certain sense of entitlement. He was, after all, born into one of the great families of the land, boasting a bona fide military hero among its ranks, to say nothing of the fact that his father might well have been prime minister but for a few ill-judged turns. As we have seen, Winston's upbringing was far from idyllic and few would envy him the experience, but he was nevertheless raised surrounded by wealth, power and influence. So what if his exam results were not what he might have hoped for? Winston was a Churchill and the Churchill men had a reputation for successfully making their way in the world.

It was soon clear that he had inherited the enviable ability to always keep one eye on the prize. Having made a decent success of his time at Sandhurst, it might have been expected that he would throw himself wholeheartedly into an army career that promised much. Instead he embarked on a most curious military existence, which ran in tandem with working as a journalist (and, by default, as a self-publicist).

His choice of regiment in 1895 is itself telling. The 4th Queen's Own Hussars was a fashionable regiment that required its officers to show some largesse in order to truly fit in. Jennie Churchill had wanted her son to look elsewhere, knowing that the family coffers were strained after her husband's death, but Winston would not budge. However, having gained entry into the exclusive club, he seemed intent on spending as little time as he could among its members.

Rather he set out on a series of international jaunts (some of which are detailed in the next chapter), operating almost as an independent soldier on occasions, with time off to hone his skills as a war correspondent – not to mention military historian and aspiring novelist. There was method behind the madness, too. 'Of course it is not my intention to become a mere professional soldier,' Churchill told Sir Felix Semon (a throat surgeon who had attempted to help alleviate some of his speech impediments) in 1896. 'I wish only to gain some experience. Some day I shall be a statesman as my father was before me.' That a life in politics was always prominent in his mind is also evidenced by a comment he made to his mother a year earlier: 'It is a fine game to play, the game of politics, and it is well worth a good hand before really plunging [in].'

It is sometimes a trait of British reserve that ambition is treated with nervous suspicion, while in other nations, for instance the USA, it is extolled as a virtue. Perhaps buoyed by his half-American ancestry, Churchill was rarely embarrassed by the grandness of his own aspiration. Returning to his old school, Harrow, in 1943, he told the boys there: 'I hope you will all nurse high thoughts in your minds, and high ambitions.'

Meanwhile, Clement Attlee – his great political opponent from the Labour ranks and the man who succeeded him as premier – recounted the following, which he claimed Churchill had said while in Number 10: 'Of course I am an egoist. Where do you get if you aren't?' Attlee doubtless believed the assertion cast Churchill in a poor light. That, though, is not to say that Churchill did not have a point: there are but a few who make a real mark in life who aren't driven to some extent by hope of their own self-aggrandizement.

Ambition burned in him even as he entered his eighth decade, with his reputation already secure as the man who had saved Britain from the Nazis. That is why the shock defeat of his Conservative Party at the first post-war general election in July 1945 stung him so badly. Looking back on those events several years later, he wrote:

I was myself deeply distressed at the prospect of sinking from a national to a party leader ... At this time I was very tired and physically so feeble that I had to be carried upstairs in a chair by the Marines from the Cabinet meetings under the Annexe. Still, I had the world position as a whole in my mind ... I could not believe this would be denied me.

If his desire to carry on in office was at this point driven primarily by a sense of duty, it is clear from these words that his ego ached at his apparent rejection by the public. (It is worth noting, too, that few analyses of that most curious of elections conclude that the result was a rejection of Churchill per se, as much as a rejection of the pre-war status quo that his party seemed to represent.)

As late as December 1953, that mixture of duty and ego are detectable in a comment he reportedly made to the son of Admiral von Tirpitz, the one-time mastermind behind the strengthening of Germany's imperial navy: 'I have no more ambitions,' Churchill said, 'but a last task I still see in front of me, which possibly nobody can take from me, is to ease world tension, to pave the way for peace and freedom.' The man who had given and achieved so much saw a final contribution he could make to the betterment of his species. But a contribution that, despite the use of the qualifying word 'possibly', he clearly believed he alone could make.

# Indulge Your Spirit of Adventure

'Live dangerously; take things as they come,
dread naught, all will be well.'

WINSTON CHURCHILL, WRITING IN THE
*DAILY MAIL* IN 1932

Churchill often had poor health, including a youthful bout of pneumonia that almost killed him. He was accident-prone, too, suffering several nasty falls and, in 1931, an almost deadly engagement with a car on a New York street. Sometimes it seemed like fate had something unhealthy in mind for him, but he was never cowed. Indeed, his many close shaves only seemed to further encourage him to tempt destiny and put himself in the way of yet more danger. The boldness and fearlessness that shone through when he was wartime leader of a nation facing stacked odds can be traced back to his much younger days.

That the nation, and every individual within it, needed to steel itself for dangerous times ahead was a theme Churchill reiterated often during the war. In 1940, for example, he wrote: '"Safety first" is the road to ruin in war, even if you had the safety, which you have not.' In the same year, Britain's bleakest in the whole conflict, he declared at a public meeting: 'This is no time for ease and comfort. It is the time to dare and endure.'

Two years later, in a private message to General Smuts

– South Africa's prime minister and a member of the War Cabinet when he was present in London – Churchill urged: 'We must not lose our faculty to dare, particularly in dark days.' Even in a speech to the Commons in September 1943, warning against recklessness, he balanced the argument by also cautioning against over-wariness: 'You have to run risks. There are no certainties in war. There is a precipice on either side of you – a precipice of caution and a precipice of over-daring.'

In short, there was little doubt in Churchill's mind that fortune favoured the brave. It was a philosophy that had guided him for many years, not least when he was commissioned into the army. In 1895, for instance, he sought special dispensation to go to Cuba in order to get a taste of military action with the Spanish forces, who at the time were engaged in the suppression of a burgeoning national liberation movement. His regiment were happy to see him off, reckoning that there was nothing so beneficial as the accumulation of real battlefield experience. Sure enough, Churchill came under enemy fire for the first time in his life, risking himself in an arena of war in which he had no real business being present.

In 1896, he was sent to India with the British Army, where he joined up with General Sir Bindon Blood's Malakand Field Force on the North-West Frontier. Again he witnessed bloody fighting up close. There followed a temporary commission with the 21st Lancers, who were operating in Sudan. While there, Churchill took a role in the last ever great cavalry charge by British forces, at the Battle of Omdurman in 1898.

Additionally, Churchill used his writing skills to capture these dramatic events and share them with a public hungry for tales of stirring adventure in distant climes. His encounters on India's North-West Frontier provided the source material for his first book, while his time in Sudan was split between soldiering and fulfilling his contractual commitments to the *Morning Post*.

After resigning his commission with the army in 1899, he promptly set off for more adventures, this time to South Africa, where the Second Anglo-Boer War was raging. Again, he was well remunerated by the *Morning Post* for regular dispatches from the front. Churchill loved adventure for its own sake (he would not have put himself in the firing line so often if he did not), but he was also keen to see that his adventures were properly documented and shared. That is to say, he was a brave adventurer who was happy for the world to know him as a brave adventurer.

Even as an established politician of national standing, there were instances when he could not resist the urge to 'get stuck in', regardless of the danger. In 1911, a crime spree by a gang of disgruntled Latvian émigrés ended in a gunfight in the East End of London that became known as the Siege of Sidney Street. His curiosity piqued, Home Secretary Churchill turned up at the scene in top hat and fur-lined coat and became an inevitable focus of attention in a highly charged situation. He would later admit: 'I should have done better to have remained quietly in my office.'

Then, a short way into the First World War in October 1914, he was present at the Siege of Antwerp, where a combined force of British, French and Belgian troops sought to repel invading German forces. Churchill sensationally suggested to the prime minister, Herbert Asquith, that he might resign as First Lord of the Admiralty if given sufficient military rank to take personal control of the city's defence. It was an offer quickly refused, but one that prompted amazement and chagrin among several of his colleagues. Churchill perhaps saw the opportunity of his own 'Blenheim', where others instead saw a man who was willing to turn his back on his existing duties when he had the scent of adventure (and personal glory) in his nostrils.

In one of his regular letters home to his mother from South Africa in 1900, Churchill provided arguably our most vivid insight into his attitude to risk: 'You must put your head into the lion's mouth if the performance is to be a success.' Hardly the words a mother longs to hear from their child on the battle lines far away, but a principle to which Churchill largely kept throughout his long and illustrious career.

## THE GREAT ESCAPE

'I have decided to escape from your custody. I have every confidence in the arrangements I have made with my friends outside ...'

WINSTON CHURCHILL, IN A LETTER TO THE SOUTH AFRICAN SECRETARY OF WAR, 1899

In a life punctuated by extraordinary incidents, the story of Churchill's escape from a Boer prisoner-of-war camp in 1899 still has the ability to astound. In his inimitable way, Churchill made sure the details were properly presented to the public. It reads like a true 'boy's own' adventure story and would ensure Churchill's fame throughout Britain and the Empire as a man of heroic courage.

He had recently made his first unsuccessful attempt to secure a seat in the House of Commons, but lost the by-election in Oldham. Thus licking his wounds, he negotiated a lucrative contract with the *Morning Post* to report on the goings-on in South Africa between the British and Boer forces. He sailed for Cape Town in October with a plan to attach himself to the yeomanry on his arrival. Not for the first time, it was unclear whether Churchill was principally soldier or journalist.

However, before he had a chance to sign up, Churchill was caught by Boer forces. The situation was serious to say the least – he might easily have been dispatched with a bullet by a disgruntled enemy officer. But Churchill was not to be bullied. He argued that he was a journalist and therefore did not qualify to be seized as a prisoner of war. The arresting officer was uncertain of his ground but decided to transport Churchill to Pretoria as a prisoner.

Churchill and two fellow captives (one Aylmer Haldane and a Sergeant Major Brockie) came up with an audacious plan of escape. It was, in truth, fairly rudimentary: the three would scale a wall into a garden and then make a run for it. Churchill, who admitted to feeling near paralysed with fear, was the first to make it over the wall. After about an hour, he realized his co-escapees would not be making an appearance (they called off their attempts owing to the guards being suspicious that something was up). So Winston was left to make his own way to freedom – or at the very least, to try.

What followed was an epic cross-country escapade that involved Churchill smuggling himself on to trains, hiding down mines and secreting himself in a van laden with wool. A week and a half after scaling his prison wall, he found himself in the safety of the British Consulate in Lourenço Marques in Portuguese East Africa (now Maputo, capital of Mozambique). From there he found a ship headed for Durban, which was safely under British rule. The Boer authorities, meanwhile, had widely circulated a 'Wanted' poster that offered a £25 bounty for his capture.

Perhaps the most remarkable aspect of the whole tale is the letter that Churchill sent to Mr De Souza, the Secretary of War for the South African Republic. It was dated 10 December (two days before the break out), and in it Churchill talked of his plans and even reflected on his treatment as a prisoner. As related in his 1900 account of his Boer adventures, *London to Ladysmith Via Pretoria*, it said:

> Sir,– I have the honour to inform you that as I do not consider that your Government have any right to detain me as a military prisoner, I have decided to escape from your custody. I have every confidence in the arrangements I have made with my friends outside, and I do not therefore expect to have another opportunity of seeing you.

Churchill went on to say that he felt well treated as a prisoner, and promised that he would testify to this when he returned to British lines. He even wanted to personally thank Dr Souza for his civility and hoped to meet in Pretoria, albeit under more favourable circumstances. He signed the letter, 'Regretting that I am unable to bid you a more ceremonious or personal farewell … Winston Churchill.' As an example of old-fashioned British pluck in the face of adversity, you'd have to go quite a distance to match it.

While lesser souls might have decided to head for the safety of home after arriving in Durban, Churchill was instead primed for the next adventure. He promptly enlisted with the South African Light Horse Brigade, spending six months in their service. It was not until July

1900 that he finally returned to England, bringing to an end five years of international adventuring and marking the start of his serious political career.

# Know How to Spin a Yarn

'I have always earned my living by my pen
and by my tongue.'

WINSTON CHURCHILL, ON THE OCCASION OF
HIS 80TH BIRTHDAY CELEBRATIONS, 1954

The South Africa escape sealed Churchill's celebrity, but he had been becoming a well-known figure at home and abroad for some time – not least because he was such an effective narrator of his own escapades. He was not a man who could be accused of playing down his achievements.

From his years of adventure between 1895 and 1900, he mined content to fulfil lucrative contracts with newspapers or for inclusion in books of his own a little further down the line. It was not always an easy task to balance his duties as a serving officer with those of an embedded journalist, but it was worthwhile. By doing so, he not only filled his personal coffers but also raised his public profile, something upon which he was intent with an eye to his longer-term political goals. When the *Daily Telegraph* printed a selection of his letters from the North-West Frontier as from 'A Young Officer', Churchill was incensed. He wrote to his mother complaining about the situation, telling her that those dispatches had been undertaken with 'a design … of bringing my personality before the electorate'.

By 1900, Churchill was not only an extremely well-paid writer, but a much sought-after public speaker as well. That year he began a lecture tour that took in large parts of the UK and the USA, and ran well into 1901. But it was not all about the money. He had a heartfelt passion for the English language and developed a distinctive voice that served him well throughout his long life. Of course, not everything he wrote was of the highest quality. There were times when it was clear he was fulfilling a commission rather than labouring for the love of it. Nonetheless, looking at his literary output in the round, Churchill emerges as both a skilled storyteller and notable stylist – attributes that would come to the fore in his guise as wartime orator. As he wrote in *My Early Life*: 'I had picked up a wide vocabulary and had a liking for words and for the feel of words fitting and falling into their places like pennies in a slot.'

On another occasion, in an address to the Authors' Club in London in 1908, he said: 'And what a noble medium the English language is. It is not possible to write a page without experiencing positive pleasure at the richness and variety, the flexibility and the profoundness of our mother tongue.' It is little surprise, then, that he looked to the giants of the language to inspire him. 'English literature is a glorious inheritance which is open to all,' he said in 1949, describing its finest writers as purveyors of 'great riches and treasures', with the King James Bible and the works of Shakespeare standing alone on the highest platform.

**MASTER INVENTOR**

Churchill, like his hero, Shakespeare, was known to invent a word or two of his own. For instance, ahead of his high-level meeting with Stalin in 1953, he is credited with inventing the word 'summit'. He is also said to have helped 'quisling' come into popular usage as a synonym for a traitor (Vidkun Quisling having been the fascist military officer who became minister-president of German-occupied Norway in 1942).

Churchill, a man who devoured books of quotations, was not averse to a little gentle 'recycling' either. For instance, his 'blood, toil, tears and sweat' speech has distinct echoes of one given by Garibaldi to his revolutionary troops in Rome almost a century earlier. In addition, he looked for stylistic templates in his wider reading. For all that Lord Macaulay was a bounder who had besmirched the family name, for example, Churchill still recognized him as 'a master of paragraphing'.

There were some literary efforts of his own that Churchill would rather had been forgotten, too. His one foray into fiction, for instance, was a potboiler called *Savrola*, published in 1900. 'I have consistently urged my friends to abstain from reading it,' he revealed many years later. But the occasional failure aside, there are few writer–speakers in English who had quite such a way with a phrase. Just as he would emerge as a skilled painter, his language was often visual, and masterfully evocative. Take this line he used in conversation with the then prime minister, Herbert Asquith, about the prospects for the war in December 1914: 'Are there not other alternatives than sending our armies to *chew barbed wire* in Flanders?' There is a grisly expressiveness to the phrase 'to *chew barbed wire*' that makes his point resonate so powerfully.

He sought to keep the standard of language high even in official documentation. Considering the reams of paperwork he had to survey, it is easy to imagine his frustration at that special form of English used by the professional bureaucrat. In a memorandum to his government colleagues in 1940, he demanded:

> Let us have an end of such phrases as these: 'It is also of importance to bear in mind the following considerations …' or 'Consideration should be given to the possibility of carrying into effect …' Most of these woolly phrases are mere padding, which can be left out altogether or replaced by a single word. Let us not shrink from using the short expressive phrase, even if it is conversational.

He once memorably railed against the verbosity of the civil service, sending a note to his Foreign Secretary, Anthony Eden, complaining that, 'It is sheer laziness not compressing thought into a reasonable space.'

**WICKED WIT**

If he was a stickler for good English, he also enjoyed having fun with it. He was a master of the pun in all its forms, and wheeled out his pun-gun in a variety of contexts. So his hencoop went by the title of 'Chickenham Palace', while he introduced into public life the word 'Admiralissimo', which was to serve as the naval equivalent of the military 'Generalissimo'. And of course there were the wisecracks, as when he pondered whether, given that a worthy person receives a peerage, should an unworthy one not receive a disappearage?

It is often said that to be able to break the rules effectively, you must know what the rules are in the first place. That is certainly true of Churchill and English. He played with the language because he loved and understood it so deeply. In his 1908 speech to the Authors' Club, he gave a hint of his complete passion for the written word. He described an idyllic scene, sitting at one's table on a sunny morning, with four clear hours ahead of you, a supply of crisp white paper and a Squeezer pen (a type of fountain pen). This, he told his audience, amounted to 'true happiness'.

## FROM HACK TO NOBEL LAUREATE

> 'Words are the only things that last for ever.'
>
> WINSTON CHURCHILL, 1938

Churchill, then, was always serious about good English and maintaining a high standard in his literary output. However, few who read the front-line dispatches from 'the pen for hire' of 1900 (and even fewer who had waded through *Savrola*) would have had him down as a future winner of the Nobel Prize for Literature. There were undoubtedly times when Churchill was, in the best sense of the word, a hack. For instance, during the 1930s, when he found himself significantly sidelined in politics, he rattled off some 400 articles, many of which his wife felt did him and his skills little justice.

Nor was Winston under any illusions about the journalistic profession. On a trip to Canada with his son in 1929, he observed: 'Fancy cutting down those beautiful trees we saw this afternoon to make pulp for those bloody newspapers, and calling it civilization.' In an article for the *Strand Magazine* three years later, he expanded on his attitudes to the press. 'The newspapers do an immense amount of thinking for the average man and woman,' he wrote. 'In fact, they supply them with such a continuous stream of standardized opinion ... that there is neither the need nor the leisure for personal reflection. All this is but a part of a tremendous educating process. But it is an education which passes in at one ear and out at the other. It is an education at once universal and superficial.'

However, alongside the articles and opinion pieces that kept Winston in cigars and fine food, he had his parallel career as a noted military and political historian and memoirist. Multi-volume works such as *The World Crisis* and *Marlborough: His Life and Times* are major achievements, and even the autobiographical *My Early Life* has much to recommend it. However, it was *The Second World War*, that astonishing retrospective of the conflict with Churchill as both historian and eyewitness, that elevated him. In 2.5 million words (written, let it not be forgotten, while he doubled up as first Leader of the Opposition and then prime minister), he produced a historical-cultural artefact that remains greatly admired.

The Nobel Prize awarding committee had considered Churchill for the literature award several times before he eventually received it in 1953. A report for the committee produced in the 1940s considered him a significant historian but not one, perhaps, whose work was so important or sparklingly literary that it warranted the grandest of all prizes. However, it was then suggested that he did make the grade if one considered his work as a speaker as well. In terms of oratory, there was simply no one who came close to matching him. And of course, his gifts as a speech-maker were worthy of appreciation not merely on an aesthetic level but for their role in defeating Nazism, too.

With *The Second World War* (or at least most of it – the last volume appeared in 1954) to his name, it was getting harder to justify the argument that Churchill was not now an important literary figure. So, after years of his name being mooted, he was finally given the great accolade. The official citation proclaimed that the prize had been awarded for 'his mastery of historical and biographical description as well as for brilliant oratory in defending exalted human values'.

Churchill could not be present at the awards ceremony itself (he was in Bermuda meeting the American president and French prime minister – a more than passable excuse for non-attendance). So Clementine delivered an acceptance speech on his behalf:

The roll on which my name has been inscribed represents much that is outstanding in the world's literature of the twentieth century … I am proud, but also awestruck at your decision to include me. I do hope you are right … But I shall have no misgivings if you have none.

Ever the great communicator, it hit just the right note of humility and pride combined.

If not every word that Churchill spoke or uttered was 'great', his lifetime's literary and oratorical output was. He continued the quote that appears at the beginning of this section thus: 'The most tremendous monuments of prodigies of engineering crumble under the hand of

Time ... but words spoken two or three thousand years ago remain with us now, not as mere relics of the past, but with all their pristine vital force.' There is every chance that his words – written and spoken – will themselves pass down through the centuries and millennia.

> 'The words and deeds of Winston Churchill will form part of the rich heritage of our nation and for our times for as long as history comes to be written and to be read.'
>
> **PRIME MINISTER HAROLD WILSON, 1965**

# Find Your Perfect Partner-in-Crime

'I married and lived happily ever afterwards.'

WINSTON CHURCHILL IN *MY EARLY LIFE*, 1930

Responding to the birth of Elizabeth II's first child, Prince Charles, in November 1948, Churchill commented: 'There is no doubt that it is around the family and the home that all the greatest virtues, the most dominating virtues of human society, are created, strengthened and maintained.'

That was quite a statement coming from someone whose home life had been so complicated and unfulfilling as a child. Yet, however troubling his early family dynamics had been, it did not stop him from seeking out a wife of his own with whom to build a new family. It has often been said that behind every great man there is a great woman. It is certainly a statement that holds true for Churchill – despite the wealth of attributes he possessed, it is unlikely that his career trajectory would have taken the course it did without the influence of his lifelong partner-in-crime, Clementine (affectionately known as Clemmie).

Intelligent and strong-willed, she provided him with unqualified support in public while in private she challenged him to be and do the best that he could. Churchill was by no means a feminist, however. His attitude to the Suffragette movement, especially in its early days, varied between mildly patronizing and unsympathetic to open hostility. Meanwhile, Nancy Astor, the first female MP, also recalled that Churchill would not converse with her when they met in the Houses of Parliament. When she challenged him on this, he responded that seeing her there made him feel as if a woman had walked into his bathroom when he had nothing but a sponge to protect himself. Yet when it came to finding the woman with whom he would spend the rest of his life, he opted for someone with a profound inner strength and a streak of real independence.

Perhaps Churchill was simply unable to resist the chemistry. 'Where does the family start?' he pondered in 1950. 'It starts with a young man falling in love with a girl. No superior alternative has yet been found!'

---

### FOLLOW YOUR HEART

As strong and enduring as their relationship was, Clementine was not Churchill's first love. That honour fell to society beauty Pamela Plowden. Then came Violet Asquith, daughter of Prime Minister Herbert Asquith, with whom Clemmie somewhat overlapped. Churchill revealed that he and Violet were not far short of engaged, and he may well have ended up with her if Clementine had refused his marriage proposal. Violet was distraught to find herself, as she saw it, jilted and not unreasonably refused to go to Winston's wedding.

---

Clemmie was undoubtedly 'the one'. Winston and she, some ten years his junior, married in 1908. The marriage, according to Churchill, writing in a *News of the World* article in 1935, 'was much the most fortunate and joyous event which happened to me in the whole of my life, for what can be more glorious than to be united in one's walk through life with a being incapable of an ignoble thought?' The couple would go on to have five children: Diana (born 1909), Randolph (1911), Sarah (1914), Marigold (1918) and Mary (1922).

Their family life, though, was not to be one of unbridled happiness. Marigold died from septicaemia when she was just two, while Diana also predeceased Winston, committing suicide in 1963 by taking an overdose of sleeping pills. Clemmie would suffer the loss of another of her children, Randolph, who died of a heart attack aged just fifty-seven, a few years after Winston's death. There were inevitably other domestic crises involving the children, including unhappy marriages and problems with alcohol.

Furthermore, the parenting styles of both Winston and Clemmie had some unfortunate echoes of Winston's own upbringing. Inevitably, his professional life took him away from the family for long spells, so Clemmie was the principal carer, but could be somewhat distant. Winston, meanwhile, dreamed of a bright future for his eldest son, Randolph, compensating for his frequent absences by thoroughly spoiling him. Randolph, though, might have been better served by being given a little more guidance and self-discipline. In adulthood, he struggled in both his personal and professional lives. In a case of history repeating itself, Winston (whom Randolph idolized just as Winston had his own father a generation earlier) came down hard on him, telling him in 1929: 'You appear to be leading a perfectly useless existence.'

Nonetheless, the relationship between Winnie and Clemmie was heartfelt and robust. If they failed to create the perfect family, then they join the ranks of millions. Perhaps, though, they should be celebrated for sticking together through the thick and thin that every family goes through. A notable achievement under normal circumstances, but even more so when one half of the couple is carving out a career that will see him considered among the greats of his age.

## CLEMMIE

'I always feel so overwhelmingly in your debt, if there can be accounts in love …'

**WINSTON CHURCHILL, WRITING TO HIS WIFE IN 1935**

Clementine Churchill was born on 1 April 1885. Like her husband-to-be, she came into the world in one of its more exclusive addresses, in London's Mayfair. She was the daughter of Sir Henry and Lady Blanche (Oglivy) Hozier – or at least, that is what the official documentation says. Lady Blanche was known for partaking in extra-marital affairs and there remains serious doubt whether Sir Henry was Clementine's father after all – a doubt Clemmie herself harboured.

Clementine met Winston briefly in 1904 but it was not until they were reunited at a dinner party four years later that their relationship blossomed. Clemmie was strikingly good-looking and engaging company. She later admitted that she was overcome by his 'dominating charm and brilliancy' – it would seem poor Violet Asquith never stood a chance. Winston and Clementine were engaged in August 1908 and married the following month at St. Margaret's Church in Westminster. A sense of Winston's feelings for his bride shine through in a letter he sent to her mother, Blanche, in which he humbly admitted his lack of wealth and standing, but focused on the love he and Clemmie bore for each other, which he felt was enough to build a marriage on. He assured Blanche he would make her daughter happy and see she received everything commensurate with her beauty and virtues.

The Churchills' marriage was incredibly resilient given the pressures exerted by Winston's prominent position in public life, and was always marked by genuine affection. This is a fact attested to by an extant correspondence of some 1,700 items between the two. He would address her as Kat while he was known as Pug (and, as an alternative, Pig). He recognized that she was his perfect foil, offering him sound advice (which, like any husband

## DAME CLEMMIE

While Clementine stood solidly behind her husband as his career progressed, she was never going to be the sort of wife who would sink into the shadows. She had far too much energy and drive for that.

During the First World War, for instance, she organized a canteen service for munitions workers in London, a job that earned her a CBE in 1918. In the Second World War, she spearheaded aid programmes for the Red Cross and the Young Women's Christian Association, as well as chairing the Fulmer Chase Maternity Hospital for Wives of Junior Officers. After the war she was made Dame Clementine Churchill GBE and took a seat in the House of Lords. As can be seen, she was every bit as formidable as her esteemed husband.

worth their salt, he did not always take) and proving herself an extremely good judge of character.

It is likely that their marriage was for long stretches not enormously physical. They had separate bedrooms for much of it and Churchill even once claimed he was able to maintain his extraordinary energy levels because he did not 'waste my essence in bed'. Nonetheless, he regarded her as his truly beloved. In return, she moulded much of her life to fit his – as was the expected custom of the time – looking after home and family while he progressed his career.

However, she was strong-willed and was quite prepared to stand up to him when she thought he had gone off course. For instance, she took an opposing view to his over the 1936 abdication saga (King Edward VIII desired to marry Wallis Simpson, an American divorcee, prompting a constitutional crisis). Winston gave his old friend Edward a sympathetic hearing and sought, unsuccessfully, to help the monarch find a route out of the situation. Clementine was rather more sanguine, and in tune with public opinion, believed that the king's primary duty was to the Crown and not to his personal feelings. As one who herself had sacrificed much already for the public good, it is a view she had every right to hold.

Even during the war she remained content to criticize Winston if she felt it was needed. Ahead of the 1945 election, she attempted to persuade him to curb the rhetoric of his 'Gestapo speech' that many believe backfired and contributed to the Conservatives' defeat (see 'See Which Way the Wind is Blowing'). Nor was she much in favour of Churchill's return for a second spell as premier six years later, presumably feeling they had done more than their bit. Sometimes her frustrations were even known to turn to violence – on one notable occasion she hurled a dish of spinach at her husband.

Like any marriage, there were sometimes more serious strains, too. When Winston descended into one of his black moods following the election defeat of 1945, Clementine wrote to her daughter Mary. She despondently described how instead of helping each other, they would argue. She selflessly accepted the blame, but admitted to finding it tough to manage with her husband and his unhappiness.

But really theirs was a marriage that prospered in what were often the most trying circumstances. As he wrote to her in a letter in 1935: 'Time passes swiftly, but is it not joyous to see how great and growing is the treasure we have gathered together, amid the storms and stresses of so many eventful and to millions tragic and terrible years?'

Clementine died in London in December 1977. She was not merely the wife of a great man, but an extraordinary woman in her own right. As Winston put it in a letter that was to be sent to her in the event of his death in the First World War: 'You have taught me how noble a woman's heart can be.'

# Refine Your Ideology

'When civilization reigns in any country, a wider
and less harassed life is afforded to the masses of
the people. The traditions of the past are cherished,
and the inheritance bequeathed to us by former
wise or valiant men becomes a rich estate to
be enjoyed and used by all …'

WINSTON CHURCHILL IN A SPEECH AT THE
UNIVERSITY OF BRISTOL, 1938

Churchill's career was marked by his ability to adapt. To some of his colleagues, this amounted to slipperiness. He was, after all, a man who entered Parliament as a Conservative in 1900, swapped sides to the Liberals in 1904 and slunk back into the Tory ranks in 1924. To some he was the ultimate vacillator. Needless to say, though, there were more nuances in his actions than that. Yes, he was in some respects an opportunist, realizing where his interests were best served at any given time. Nor could it ever be said he was a great 'party man'. He was a politician who believed less in how he could serve a party than how it could serve him.

Yet for all that, Churchill developed a well-defined political ideology. Some of it may be on the more unpalatable side today, rooted as it often was in Victorian imperial ideals, but he should perhaps not be judged too harshly for being a product of his time. However, another strand of Churchill was distinctly radical and egalitarian, a fact that now often goes unrecognized.

Striving to briefly encapsulate his philosophy, which evolved and occasionally somersaulted in a political career that extended from the reign of Queen Victoria to that of

Queen Elizabeth II, is surely a fool's errand. Nonetheless, there are a few strands that we can pick out as dominating his thinking for the duration of his career. Foremost of these were his belief in the intrinsic strength and value of British democratic ideals and a faith in his nation's essential 'fairness' (imperfect as it sometimes was, a fact even he could admit). Allied to this was the deeply held conviction that the British Empire was a good thing and that the spread of British principles was beneficial to the world as a whole.

Then there was his commitment to the equality of opportunity. Despite being high-born himself, he recognized that the future of the nation depended on the masses being guaranteed a minimum standard of living, but without putting any limit on how high anyone might rise by their own efforts.

'In the coming years, many in countless words will strive to interpret the motives, describe the accomplishments, and extol the virtues of Winston Churchill – soldier, statesman, and citizen that two great countries were proud to claim as their own. Among all the things so written or spoken, there will ring out through all the centuries one incontestable refrain: Here was a champion of freedom.'

FORMER U.S. PRESIDENT,
DWIGHT D. EISENHOWER, 1965

Underpinning these beliefs was his determination that 'civilization' should reign. That is to say, every member of society should be treated decently and they in turn should treat others decently. Crucially, he believed that those in power should be subject to particular scrutiny. In a speech to the House of Commons shortly before the outbreak of the war in 1939, he described what he considered the word 'civilization' to mean:

the freedom to criticize the government of the day; free speech; free press; free thought; free religious observance; no racial persecution; fair treatment of minorities; and courts of law and justice which have an authority independent of the executive and untainted by party bias.

Churchill has often been depicted as a flag-waving jingoist, but it is an image that tells only half the story. He was undoubtedly patriotic, and his wartime role required that he play up this particular aspect of his credo. However, his patriotism was not blind. His love for his country was based on a belief that it had attained what he called in 1938 'the blessings of civilization'. It was a conclusion he had reached in part through his wide reading of history. 'There is freedom; there is law; there is love of country … there is a widening prosperity,' he told an audience in Bristol that year. 'There are measured opportunities of correcting abuses and making further progress.'

Britain in the early twentieth century was not

a paradise: the long-established class system could be stifling, and for those who found themselves at the bottom of the social ladder, poverty was a savage reality. While there was a degree of meritocracy, if you possessed the wrong name or accent or background, your chances of social advancement were undeniably limited. The First World War would further diminish parts of the social fabric, with the general population turning away in large numbers from both faith in God and in those charged with governing them. In a country where foreign faces remained largely unfamiliar outside of pockets of the largest metropolises and trading ports, there was an inherent distrust of alien 'otherness', too.

But still, when compared to many of its international rivals, the country embraced a certain level of social progressiveness. If it was difficult to dig your way out of real poverty, it was not so difficult for those in the ever-expanding middle class to establish a decently comfortable life for themselves through a combination of hard work and talent. There was provision for a rudimentary education for all as well, and countless social organs that sought to better the lot of the poor (if not always altogether successfully). Crucially, Britain was a well-functioning parliamentary democracy – its leaders could be brought to task and, if necessary, removed from office by the popular vote.

Churchill proclaimed ahead of the 1945 general election: 'I have an invincible confidence in the genius of Britain. I believe in the instinctive wisdom of our well-tried democracy.' This was not merely the rhetoric of electioneering, but a deeply held conviction. It was also why Churchill believed in Britain's entitlement to secure and govern a global empire. Empire is rarely an altruistic undertaking: for Britain, it was a means to secure supplies of raw materials and commodities and to safeguard its export routes. However, there had long been a narrative of empire that held Britain as an improving influence, civilizing the 'savage'. Churchill was brought up on this notion and remained married to it for the rest of his life. As we shall see, for instance, his not entirely rational low opinion of Gandhi went hand-in-hand with a genuine concern for the future prospects of the subcontinent. As he would say in a speech to the Canada Club in London in April 1939: 'If the British Empire is fated to pass from life into history, we must hope it will not be by the slow process of dispersion and decay, but in some supreme exertion for freedom, for right and for truth.'

Weighted against Churchill the patriotic supporter of empire was Churchill the radical social reformer. This aspect of his politics shone through in the years immediately after his defection from the Conservatives to the Liberals in 1904. In this period he was a staunch ally of David Lloyd George who, as Chancellor from 1908 until 1915, was the driving force behind a package of game-changing welfare legislation implemented by the Asquith administration.

The aim was for the government to guarantee every individual a 'minimum standard' of living and to provide a framework for meritocratic advancement. Churchill outlined the vision to an audience in Glasgow in 1906: 'We want to draw a line below which we will not allow persons to live and labour, yet above which they may compete with all the strength of their manhood. We want to have free competition upwards; we decline to allow free competition to run downwards.'

Churchill was never, it need hardly be said, a socialist. He was a believer in free trade and was an instinctive opponent of protectionism. Equally, he fought against any talk of nationalization of industry (in peacetime, anyway) and had little stomach for an organized programme of wealth distribution. But he did believe in the right of ordinary people to have a decent quality of life.

Thus he delivered a string of speeches in 1909 that sounded as if they had been written not by an aristocratic Old Harrovian, but by an enthusiastic new recruit to the emerging Labour Party. 'We think that the supremacy and the predominance of our country depend upon the maintenance of the vigour and health of its population, just as its true glory must always be found in the happiness of its cottage homes,' he said in one speech that year.

In an address in Leicester earlier in the year, he launched an attack on income inequality:

It is there you will find the seeds of imperial ruin and national decay – the unnatural gap between rich and poor, the divorce of the people from the land, the want of proper discipline and training in our youth … the constant insecurity in the means of subsistence and employment which breaks the heart of many a sober, hard-working man, the absence of any established minimum standard of life and comfort among the workers, and, at the other end, the swift increase of vulgar, joyless luxury – here are the enemies of Britain.

A few months later, he was at it again, this time to an audience in Manchester:

I think it is our duty to use the strength and the resources of the state to arrest the ghastly waste, not merely of human happiness, but of national health and strength which follows when a working man's home which has taken him years to get together is broken up and scattered through a long spell of unemployment, or when, through the death, the sickness or the invalidity of the bread-winner, the frail boat in which the fortunes of the family are embarked founders, and the women and children are left to struggle helplessly on the dark waters of a friendless world.

One could point to, say, his unsympathetic attitude to the General Strikers in 1926 as evidence that Churchill's period of radical egalitarianism was short-lived. However, on that occasion, it may be argued, his actions were motivated more by a dislike of unregulated mass public protest (something he also found unpalatable in the Suffragette movement) rather than fundamental antipathy to the strikers' cause.

As wartime leader, he would strive again to secure a decent standard of home-front life for all. His attitude is also evident in a speech he broadcast in January 1950 as Leader of the Opposition: 'All parties are agreed that the prevention of unemployment ranks next to food in the duties of any government.'

Belief in the pre-eminence of British 'civilization', commitment to the imperial project, advocation for a social 'safety net' beneath a meritocratic ladder of social progression – these were the three fundamental pillars of the Churchillian political ethos.

## CHURCHILL, CONSERVATISM AND LIBERALISM

'Anyone can rat, but it takes a certain ingenuity to re-rat.'

WINSTON CHURCHILL ON RETURNING TO THE CONSERVATIVES IN 1924

Given that Winston's father had been a Conservative Chancellor of the Exchequer, it was little surprise that he initially pinned his colours to the same mast. However, after taking his seat in Parliament in 1900, he spent the next four years making enemies within his own party by launching attacks on a number of policy areas, but especially over tariff reform. Churchill believed in free trade all of his life, and it was this issue that proved decisive in his crossing the Commons to the Liberal benches in 1904 (a deal no doubt sweetened by promises of career advancement in a future Liberal government). In 1907, for instance, he told the Commons in a debate on protectionism '… taxes are an evil – a necessary evil, but still an evil, and the fewer we have of them the better.'

Churchill's utter disillusion with the Conservatives at this time is indicated in a letter (unsent in the event) written to a friend in 1903, a few months before his defection. 'I am an English Liberal,' he wrote. 'I hate the Tory party, their men, their words and their methods.'

The move to the Liberals seemed to suit him. Domestically, as described in the previous section, he carried out some of his most important work in a potent alliance forged with Lloyd George. Always an advocate of personal liberty, as President of the Board of Trade from 1908 to 1910 he organized labour exchanges and championed unemployment insurance. Whereas he believed socialism sought to 'pull down wealth', the Liberals he argued 'raise up poverty'. He set out his take on the Liberal position in a 1906 speech in Glasgow:

> Liberalism supplies at once the higher impulse and the practicable path … it proceeds by courses of moderation. By gradual steps, by steady effort from day to day, from year to year, liberalism enlists

hundreds of thousands upon the side of progress and popular democratic reform whom militant socialism would drive into violent Tory reaction. That is why the Tory Party hate us.

His resignation as First Lord of the Admiralty after the Dardanelles incident in 1915 was an obvious low point, but he was brought back into Lloyd George's wartime coalition in 1917. As post-war Secretary of State for the Colonies, he was pleased to be able to pursue a path to home rule in Ireland, a concept that was anathema to many in the Conservative ranks. Churchill was crucial to securing the 1921 Anglo-Irish Treaty that divided the island of Ireland between the Irish Free State and British-ruled Northern Ireland. Michael Collins, the famed Irish revolutionary leader, was even prompted to comment: 'Tell Winston we could have done nothing without him.'

Yet within a year it had all gone wrong for Churchill and the Liberals. The party was out of government, with no Liberal tasting power until the Liberal Democrats entered into coalition as the junior party to the Conservatives in 2010. Churchill lost his seat, finding himself out of the Commons after twenty-two years. He did stand for the party again but was unable to claim a seat. The Liberals, it was apparent, were a waning force in British politics, and so began the drawn-out process of Churchill's reuniting with the Conservatives. He unsuccessfully fought one by-election as an independent and won another as a 'Constitutionalist' backed by the Tories.

The flirtation soon heated up. He told Sir Robert Horne, a leading Tory: 'I am what I have always been – a Tory democrat. Force of circumstance has compelled me to serve with another party, but my views have never changed, and I should be glad to give effect to them by rejoining the Conservatives.' He did just that, becoming Chancellor in the Conservative government of Stanley Baldwin in November 1924. But when Labour formed the next government after electoral victory in 1929, Churchill was all but sidelined by the party grandees for a decade and more. Baldwin was among the attack dogs, saying in 1936:

When Winston was born, lots of fairies swooped down on his cradle with gifts – imagination, eloquence, industry, ability. And then came a fairy who said, 'No one person has the right to so many gifts,' picked him up and gave him such a shake and twist that with all the gifts he was denied judgement and wisdom.

It is telling, too, that Churchill became prime minister before party leader, with many of the Tory rank and file favouring Lord Halifax for the role of wartime premier. In October 1940, he would reassure the party faithful who had just elected him party leader:

Am I by temperament and conviction able sincerely to identify myself with the main historical conceptions of Toryism, and can I do justice to them and give expression to them spontaneously in speech and action? I have always faithfully served two public causes which I think stand supreme – the maintenance of the enduring greatness of Britain and her empire and the historical continuity of our island life.

However, in the build-up to the 1945 general election, there was renewed blurring of his loyalties. In a remarkable election broadcast that June, he said: 'There is scarcely a Liberal sentiment which animated the great Liberal leaders of the past which we [Conservatives] do not inherit and defend.' Clementine, herself at heart a Liberal, always felt he was more at home with that party than among the Tories.

There was undeniable expediency in his decisions to change parties. He established himself on the political scene with the Conservatives, the party of his father, but moved to the Liberals and was quickly rewarded with high office, becoming Home Secretary in 1910. In 1922, the Liberals were a spent force, so he returned to the Conservatives and was again rewarded with one of the great offices of state: Chancellor of the Exchequer. Perhaps the truth is that Churchill was such a maverick and a believer in individual freedom that party structures simply did not suit him. It is easy to argue that he was happiest and most constructive working in wartime coalitions of 'all the talents'. He might best be described as a conservative with liberal tendencies, or alternatively a liberal with conservative tendencies. The exact balance was in an almost constant state of flux.

# Roll with
# the Punches

'When we face with a steady eye the difficulties
which lie before us, we may derive new
confidence from remembering those we
have already overcome.'

WINSTON CHURCHILL IN A BROADCAST, 1941

Politics can be a rough-and-tumble business, and over a career as long as Churchill's, it was inevitable that he would find himself in some tight corners. But time and again he displayed great tenacity, recovering from setbacks that would have broken lesser characters. He was living proof of the truth of the old adage that it is not about how many times you fall, but about how many times you get back up again.

His uneasy childhood gave him an education in the school of hard knocks. If it wasn't much fun at the time, they were formative experiences that served to toughen him up for later life. Learning to cope with the criticism of his own father, the disdain of teachers and the playground barbs of fellow pupils no doubt left him well prepared for the turbulence and forceful verbal sparring of Parliament. Indeed, having confronted a host of characters seemingly intent on undermining him was good practice for his face-off with Hitler.

Even into adulthood, his private life brought with it many trials. 1921, for instance, saw the devastating loss of his infant daughter, Marigold. But Winston, by then Secretary of State for the Colonies, knew that he could not let his private grief encroach on his public duty. It must have required quite an extraordinary 'stiff upper lip' to keep on going in such a high-profile role, but somehow he did. These personal tragedies also have a habit of putting into perspective one's professional travails.

After a stellar rise through the government ranks, the first great setback of his political life was the ill-fated Dardanelles campaign during the First World War. Churchill had personally pushed hard for the offensive that went so catastrophically wrong. Identified closely with the misadventure in the public's eye, he was left with little choice but to resign as First Lord of the Admiralty. Yet Churchill did not believe he had done anything wrong or even that the campaign had been ill-conceived. Instead he was convinced that the problem lay in its poor execution. In his mind, the operation might well have succeeded if his advice had been more closely followed, but ultimately, all of that was academic.

Finding himself effectively forced out of a job he loved and which afforded him great influence at a time of national crisis, the affair scarred him badly. In the years to come he would talk about what had happened in words tinged with bitterness. It was doubtless a painful experience (even today it is held up as a black mark against him by his critics) and impacted on his career to a greater or lesser degree for fully twenty-five years. Yet somehow he bounced back from the abject episode. To that extent, it may be regarded as key in his development as a figure who could cope with the downs as well as the ups of high office.

By 1917 he had been ushered back into government as Minister of Munitions by his old ally David Lloyd George, who had succeeded Herbert Asquith as premier. By the middle of the following decade he was Chancellor of the Exchequer in a Tory government. Not a bad comeback within a decade of the Dardanelles. But there were more personal crises yet to come. Principally, his isolation after leaving government in 1929, which lasted throughout the 1930s. Though not quite a lone voice, his dire warnings of the coming threat from Germany were not merely ignored by those in power but were used as evidence that Churchill was a political crank and out of touch.

But, as we all know, it quickly became apparent that there was much less in the idea that Hitler would be sated if his European neighbours simply turned a blind eye to his growing litany of outrages. When the chips were down and Britain needed a heroic redeemer, Churchill was on hand. The willingness with which he threw himself into the job was all the more remarkable considering the disdain his country had shown him since leaving office as Chancellor.

Following the end of the war, with Churchill now in his sixties and justifiably proposed by his supporters as the saviour of the free world, there were yet more indignities with which to cope. Against almost everybody's expectation, he was forced from office at the very first opportunity – the general election of July 1945. Few seriously argue it was a rejection of him as an individual (he continued to enjoy superstar status wherever he went) but it came as a serious blow. While many men of his age would likely have thrown in the towel (especially given the toll taken on his health and well-being by the war), instead he took on the duties of Leader of the Opposition and eventually returned for a second spell as prime minister. When it came to rolling with the punches, there has never been anyone quite like Churchill.

## THE DARDANELLES DISASTER

'Not to persevere – that was the crime.'

WINSTON CHURCHILL REFLECTING ON THE DARDANELLES CAMPAIGN IN 1923

The Dardanelles Campaign (also known as the Gallipoli Campaign) ranks alongside the greatest disasters in British military history. Its victims, though, were not only British, with an international force of Australian, New Zealand and French colonial troops also involved in the mission. But why was the campaign important and what went so horribly wrong?

The Dardanelles is a strait in the north–west corner of

Turkey, bordered on one side by the Gallipoli peninsula and protected by a series of forts. At the start of the First World War, the strategically important strait was under the rule of the Ottoman Empire (centred on modern-day Turkey), which had come out in support of Germany. Towards the end of 1914, the British government were discussing the possibility of attacking the Ottomans to take control of the strait, and in the process encouraging some of the latter's Balkan allies to join the Allies.

After much heated debate, during which Churchill argued strongly for the mission, the go-ahead was given. With Australian and New Zealand Army Corps (ANZAC) troops having been stationed in the region, the Allied offensive began in February 1915. An armada of Allied battleships entered the strait, but initial good progress slowed as the vessels encountered heavily mined waters. Several ships were lost or damaged, with the death toll running into hundreds.

Churchill was told by senior naval figures that there was no chance of capturing Gallipoli without the help of the army. As tens of thousands of British troops joined the forces already in place, the Ottoman authorities got wind of the imminent attack and drafted in their own troops to defend the area. The land attack began on 25 April but was unable to secure the peninsula. By the end of August over 40,000 Allied men had been lost. The request came back to London for reinforcements of nearly 100,000 more soldiers. Churchill argued it was necessary but faced opposition from senior cabinet figures, who prevailed.

Having campaigned so heartily for the assault, Churchill was indelibly linked with what had become a disaster. It was clear, also, that he lacked the support of many of his government colleagues in the issue's aftermath. In mid–May, he reluctantly resigned as First Lord of the Admiralty. It was decided to initiate the withdrawal of over 100,000 Allied troops active in the region, an operation carried out between December 1915 and January 1916. The Allies had nothing to show for their long months in Turkey, save for the loss of some 60,000 men and four times as many casualties.

While Churchill realized he had little choice but to take a public fall for the debacle, he always felt a sense of injustice regarding the Dardanelles. It was evident in his testimony in March 1917 to the Dardanelles Commission, established to look at what had transpired:

A fifth of the resources, the effort, the loyalty, the resolution, the perseverance vainly employed in the Battle of the Somme to gain a few shattered villages and a few square miles of devastated ground, would in the Gallipoli peninsula, used in time, have united the Balkans on our side, joined hands with Russia, and cut Turkey out of the war.

# Be Pragmatic …

'In life's steeplechase one must always jump
the fences when they come.'

WINSTON CHURCHILL IN *MY EARLY LIFE*, 1930

Given the great hardships he faced at different periods of his life, Churchill came to realize the value of pragmatism. He was a man of ideals and principles, but understood that they were of little worth if you could not create the circumstances in which they might be implemented.

It is somewhat ironic that his political approach may be described in terms of *Realpolitik*, a concept of German origin first described by Ludwig von Rochau in the nineteenth century. In short, Churchill was less an ideologue than a politician more at home dealing with the practical impact of government. He always set out to deal with the job in hand without being too precious. As he would say in Sheffield in 1951: '… perfect solutions [to] our difficulties are not to be looked for in an imperfect world.'

He applied pragmatism to his own life, too. It is evident in his calculated bid for fame and fortune as soldier and journalist in the period between his leaving Sandhurst and entering Parliament. And it is in even greater evidence in his changes of political party. That is not to say that there weren't moral or intellectual factors behind his actions also, but pragmatism was ever present. His trick was to have an end goal always in view and to have the patience to arrive at it by navigating the journey one step at a time.

---

**KEEP A CATCHPHRASE IN YOUR LOCKER**

Churchill's practical attitude was often neatly summed up in his various sound bites and catchphrases. So, as the war approached its end in 1945, he told the House of Commons: 'Only one link in the chain of destiny can be handled at a time.' It could have been his personal motto. In fact, 'KBO' might have sufficed, too. 'KBO' was a popular Churchillian refrain and stood for 'Keep buggering on'. It serves as a slightly fruity shorthand for his 'never give up' mindset that saw him deal with each problem as it came. Where others might have been overwhelmed, Churchill prospered in the face of adversity and strove to turn every challenge to his ultimate advantage. 'Difficulties mastered,' he would say in 1943, 'are opportunities won.'

---

Never was his pragmatism and calmness in the face of crisis so tested than during his wartime premiership.

Equally, he was never found wanting. His strength as leader of a gravely imperilled nation came in part from his acceptance of the situation as it was. He had a lifelong fascination with war and now brought a historian's perspective to conflict. In a speech to Parliament all the way back in 1901 (during the Second Boer War), he had noted: 'War is a game with a good deal of chance in it, and, from the little I have seen of it, I should say that nothing in war ever goes right, except occasionally by accident.' Then, in *My Early Life*, he wrote:

> Never, never, never believe any war will be smooth and easy, or that anyone who embarks on that strange voyage can measure the tides and hurricanes he will encounter. The Statesman who yields to war fever must realize that once the signal is given, he is no longer the master of policy but the slave of unforeseeable and uncontrollable events.

These were valuable lessons and ensured he undertook his wartime duties under no illusions about the job ahead. This no doubt added to his aura of calmness that so galvanized the population, particularly in the most perilous days of 1940. He knew that Britain was on the brink (he never understood, for instance, why the German army had not finished off the British forces at Dunkirk that year), but saw the country through successive grave episodes. By the end of the year, Britain had survived the Blitz, beaten the odds to emerge victorious in the Battle of Britain and had taken succour from the Dunkirk evacuations (arguably the most glorious retreat in military history).

His sense of what needed to be done to complete the job at hand would subsequently guide him through intensely difficult decision-making phases. For instance, he agreed to the blanket bombing of German cities not through a hunger for vengeance (as we shall see, that was rarely his style), but because he was convinced it offered the quickest path to achieving complete victory. There were difficult decisions to make on the home front, too. Take the Bethnal Green Tube disaster, the worst civilian tragedy of the war. In 1943, a stampede into the Underground station's air-raid shelter during a false alarm resulted in the deaths of 173 people. The East End of London had had more than its fair share of heartache by then, but felt especially aggrieved when the incident went virtually unreported in the national press. Churchill had influenced his newspaper-owning friends for suppression of the story, fearing that its spread could devastate the national spirit.

Such were the sometimes deeply troubling decisions he was compelled to make with the ultimate defeat of the Axis powers in mind. Like many of the greatest and most inspirational public figures, behind closed doors he was coolly calculating when he needed to be. In his history, *The Second World War*, he summed it up thus: 'In life people have first to be taught, "Concentrate on essentials."'

# … But Don't Forget Your Guiding Principles

'The only guide to a man is his conscience, the only shield to his memory is the rectitude and sincerity of his actions.'

WINSTON CHURCHILL IN A SPEECH IN THE HOUSE OF COMMONS UPON THE DEATH OF NEVILLE CHAMBERLAIN, 1940

While pragmatism is often an admirable characteristic, if it is not tempered by reference to a moral compass, it can quickly start to look very ugly indeed. For all that Churchill was prepared to make the difficult and uncompromising decisions required during the Second World War, he nonetheless clung tightly to a number of guiding principles. First among these was the preservation of the 'civilization' he so valued. It can be argued that it was in defence of 'civilization' that he was able to make decisions that in isolation could be seen as *un*civilized (war by its very nature being an uncivilized environment). In a speech he gave at London's Albert Hall in 1947, he outlined what he considered to be truly important in a society: 'All the greatest things are simple, and many can be expressed in a single word: Freedom; Justice; Honour; Duty; Mercy; Hope.' His pragmatism, then, always rested upon a moral framework.

He never lost sight of his duties as a holder of public office. As a campaigning Liberal in 1906, he had paraphrased Voltaire, telling the Commons: 'Where there is great power there is great responsibility.'

Another speech he made in Parliament thirty-one years later is also enlightening. It shows Churchill's ready grasp that war and ethics do not mix well, but that the latter should not lose out altogether. 'Moral force is, unhappily, no substitute for armed force,' he said, 'but it is a very good reinforcement …'

The 1930s – Churchill's decade in the political wilderness – found him clinging to his core principles even as they cost him personally and professionally. An isolated figure of fun who was widely characterized as a relic of the past, he simply refused to follow the groundswell of popular opinion within Westminster and the wider nation. 'I have a tendency,' he observed in 1940, 'against which I should, perhaps, be on my guard, to swim against the stream.' It was an attitude long ingrained. As far back as 1899, when he was in South Africa, he had noted: 'How few men are strong enough to stand against the prevailing currents of opinion!'

Despite the various British governments of the 1930s being bent on avoiding hostilities at all costs, Churchill stuck to his guns, consistently arguing that Hitler had to be faced down. The desire to evade war was understandable. The British were still mending after the horror of the First World War, the economy was ragged and the electorate balked at the prospect of another major conflict. But Churchill was fearful that inaction would lead only to deeper calamity. As the international community made repeated concessions to Hitler's yearning for a Greater Germany, Churchill was one of the few who realized that the more that particular beast was fed, the hungrier it became.

Far from being a relic, Churchill turned out to be at his most relevant. Where successive governments contorted themselves in a desperate bid to avoid war, Churchill brought clarity. 'Out of intense complexities, intense simplicities emerge,' he had written in *The World Crisis* in 1927. So it now proved. There was a profound courageous–ness in his willingness to say the unsayable despite the risk of ridicule. But honesty in policy making, along with circumspection, was core to his political approach.

> 'In politics, when you are in doubt what to do,
> do nothing … when you are in doubt
> what to say, say what you really think.'
>
> A SPEECH BY CHURCHILL IN
> MANCHESTER IN 1905

Nor did he seem concerned that he might find himself on the wrong side of the debate. With an illustrious career already to his name, it was as if he was now able to rise above the political rabble. If it turned out that the appeasers were on the right track after all, so be it. 'What does it matter who gets exposed or discomfited? If the country is safe, who cares for individual politicians, in or out of office?' he asked the House of Commons.

For all their admirable intentions to retain the peace, the appeasers were proven terribly wrong. For every concession Hitler won, he grew only greedier and more aggressive. Churchill would at last be recognized as a sage rather than a fool. While his arrival at 10 Downing Street was no foregone conclusion, he was a natural choice to guide the nation in war. Once in office, he set out to establish a political climate in which the normal rivalries and the scramble for personal advancement were set aside. 'I say, let pre-war feuds die; let personal quarrels be forgotten, and let us keep our hatreds for the common enemy,' he told the House of Commons in 1940. 'Let party interest be ignored, let all our energies be harnessed, let the whole ability and forces of the nation be hurled into the struggle, and let all the strong horses be pulling on the collar.' This was nothing less than a manifesto for moral government united in fighting a common enemy.

His strong belief that personal considerations had to give way in favour of the greater good is there to be seen throughout his wartime addresses. For instance, in a speech at Bradford Town Hall in December 1942, he said:

We are all of us defending something which is, I won't say dearer, but greater than country; namely, a cause. That cause is the cause of freedom and of justice, of the weak against the strong, of law against violence, of mercy and tolerance against brutality and ironbound tyranny. That is the cause we are fighting for …

Three years later he told Parliament: 'So long as I am acting from duty and conviction, I am indifferent to taunts and jeers. I think they will probably do me more good than harm.'

If war represents the failure of civilization, Churchill showed that it is at least possible for individuals to continue to strive for civility amid the maelstrom of conflict. It would be absurd to say that his life was one of selflessness. Churchill was a man of significant ego and ambition who was willing to wheel, deal and compromise in the pursuit of his aims. He was, nonetheless, a politician with a defined set of principles. Avoiding the inflexibility of the ideologue, he found a rare balance so that his pragmatism served a wider moral philosophy, and never more so than during wartime.

In the most testing of circumstances, he was at his most focused on doing the 'right thing' and harnessed that sentiment for millions of others. He expressed it perfectly in volume VI of *The Second World War*:

… for us in Britain and the British Empire, who had alone been in the struggle from the first day to the last and staked our existence on the result, there was a sublime meaning behind it all. Weary and worn, impoverished but undaunted and now triumphant, we had a moment that was sublime. We gave thanks to God for the noblest of all His blessings – the sense that we had done our duty.

Over the course of his career, Churchill was too wily and cunning an operator to be described as a 'conviction politician' (one of those modern phrases that he would probably have detested anyway). He was familiar with the politician's dark arts, most certainly. But his pragmatism was weighed against a broad desire to protect those ideals he most valued: civilization, personal liberty and democracy.

## CHURCHILL THE DEMOCRAT

'The government is the servant of the people and not its master.'

**WINSTON CHURCHILL IN A SPEECH IN NORWEGIAN PARLIAMENT, 1948**

An integral element of the 'civilization' (or at least the British take on it) that Churchill so extolled was democracy. In 1947 he would put it like this: 'Government of the people, by the people, for the people, still remains the sovereign definition of democracy.'

A lifelong advocate of democratic ideals, there was little he enjoyed more than a good tussle with his opponents in Parliament – this was democracy in action as far as he was concerned. But his role as defender of democracy took on a much more serious tone when he was cast against the fascist regimes of Hitler, Mussolini and their ilk. Democracy was no longer an abstract concept but a tangible, and imperilled, reality.

Churchill was married to his ideology, and as in any marriage there were times when he grew frustrated with his partner. His greatest complaint was that it could become complacent. In an article he wrote for the *Strand* in 1931, he argued, 'Democratic governments drift along the line of least resistance, taking short views, paying their way with sops and doles, and smoothing their path with pleasant-sounding platitudes.'

Such criticisms, though, were little more than minor quibbles. He gave a more rounded view, for instance, in a speech he made to Bermuda's House of Assembly in January 1942:

> With all their weakness and with all their strength, with all their faults, with all their virtues, with all the criticisms that may be made against them, with their many shortcomings, with lack of foresight, lack of continuity of purpose or pressure only of superficial purpose, they [democracies] nevertheless assert the right of the common people – the broad masses of people – to take a conscious and effective share in the government of their country.

When Hitler took power in Germany, Churchill soon spoke out against its anti-democratic nature. In 1934, he told the House of Commons: 'Germany is ruled by a handful of autocrats who ... have neither the long interests of a dynasty to consider, nor those very important restraints which a democratic Parliament and constitutional system impose upon any executive government.' If some of his domestic audience still needed persuasion that Hitler was bad news then, few were under any illusion by 1938. However, Churchill was by that point striving to persuade the USA to join Britain against the Nazis, while Washington was keen to leave Europe to sort out its own squabbles.

In a speech broadcast to the States that year he attempted to engage the support of America, fabled land of the free. Referring to Germany, Churchill told them:

A state of society where many may not speak their minds, where children denounce their parents to the police, where a businessman or small shopkeeper ruins his competitor by telling tales about his private opinions … cannot long endure if brought into contact with the healthy outside world.

Churchill was also astute enough to know that it is generally much harder to get a thriving democracy on to a war footing than it is to ready a state ruled by a militaristic dictator. In a wireless broadcast in October 1939, he warned: 'When a peaceful democracy is suddenly made to fight for its life, there must be a lot of trouble and hardship in the process of turning over from peace to war.' A month later he was making a similar point to Parliament:

## ... But Don't Forget Your Guiding Principles

Peaceful parliamentary countries, which aim at freedom for the individual and abundance for the mass, start with a heavy handicap against a dictatorship whose sole theme has been war, the preparation for war, and the grinding up of everything and everybody into its military machine.

Nonetheless, Europe's fascistic dictatorships did eventually tumble. There was, however, a bitter pill to swallow as they did so. While the Western democracies could claim to have been instrumental in their defeat, it was a victory that could not have been achieved without Stalin, whose own autocratic regime rivalled Hitler's for brutality and suppression. What Churchill saw as the decline of democratic liberalism during his lifetime profoundly saddened him. 'Tolerance was one of the chief features of the great liberalizing movements which were the glory of the latter part of the nineteenth century,' he told the Belgian parliament in November 1945. 'We may well recur to those bygone days, from whose standards of enlightenment, compassion, and hopeful progress the terrible twentieth century has fallen so far.'

But Churchill being Churchill, his disappointment only spurred him on. He went on a post-war mission to establish his version of democracy with as much verve as ever. Consider his championing of democratic debate to the Norwegian parliament in 1948: 'I have made myself the spokesman for the greatest possible freedom of debate even if it should lead to sharp encounters and hard words.' That speech came a few months after he had outlined to the House of Commons his vision for the democracy he wanted Britain to have:

Establish a basic standard of life and labour and provide the necessary basic foods for all. Once that is done, set the people free, get out of the way, and let them all make the best of themselves, and win whatever prizes they can for their families and for their country ... Only in this way will an active, independent, property-owning democracy be established.

# See Which Way the Wind is Blowing

'I saw it all coming and cried aloud to my own
fellow countrymen and to the world, but no
one paid any attention.'

WINSTON CHURCHILL AT WESTMINSTER
COLLEGE, FULTON, MISSOURI, 1946

The quote on the previous page refers to the Second World War and comes from the speech in which Churchill warned of the 'Iron Curtain' falling across Europe. His address continued:

> Up till the year 1933 or even 1935, Germany might have been saved from the awful fate which has overtaken her and we might all have been spared the miseries Hitler let loose upon mankind. There never was a war in all history easier to prevent by timely action than the one which has just desolated such great areas of the globe. It could have been prevented in my belief without the firing of a single shot, and Germany might be powerful, prosperous and honoured today; but no one would listen and one by one we were all sucked into the awful whirlpool.

You can hardly blame him for a touch of the 'I told you sos'. As the record shows, Churchill spent years warning his political colleagues about the risk Germany posed, only gaining their collective ear when the time to avert the danger had passed. Yet this was not the only occasion when he saw clearly what the future held while others were blind.

Throughout his career he had an uncanny knack of knowing what was coming round the corner. Perhaps it was thanks to his journalistic nose for a story, but he often seemed able to sniff out the reality of a situation more efficiently than many of his colleagues in the political classes. So, for instance, the young Churchill was quick to embrace the air age. Despite Clemmie's disapproval, he even made efforts to learn to fly in the 1910s, before an accident in 1919 brought the enterprise to an end. But it was in his capacity as an MP that he most effectively supported the development of flight. He not only suggested the creation of a British Air Service but also, in 1909, pushed the government to make contact with those aviation pioneers, the Wright brothers of America, so that Britain might be at the forefront of the flying revolution. As First Lord of the Admiralty in 1914, he founded the Royal Naval Air Service, and from 1919 to 1921 served as Secretary of State for Air. By the early 1920s he had personally approved aerial bombardment on three occasions: once against Sinn Fein operatives in Ireland, once in Iraq and once in Palestine. The air force would of course have a vital role to play in the Second World War, but Churchill had realized the potential of military and bomb-carrying aircraft decades earlier.

His willingness to embrace innovation while other more cautious types tarried was striking. He played a key role, for example, in the development of the military tank. In a wonderful note he sent to Prime Minister Herbert Asquith in January 1915, he set out plans for a rudimentary version of the apparatus that would eventually reconfigure modern warfare:

> It would be quite easy in a short time to fit up a number of steam tractors with small armoured shelters, in which men and machine guns could be placed, which would be bulletproof.

He further suggested that, if used at night, they would not be affected by artillery file, and that the caterpillar system could cross trenches with ease, the weight of the vehicle crushing any barbed wire.

His openness to new ideas continued into the Second World War as he sought to discern how the nature of conflict would evolve. It was to this end that he became acquainted with the eccentric inventor and journalist, Geoffrey Pyke, the genius behind the Habbakuk Project. Pyke's intention was to build an iceberg aircraft carrier to protect mid-Atlantic transport routes. The theory was that ice, being unsinkable, would provide total defence against traditional bomb and torpedo attacks. Any repairs would require only a supply of water and a suitably cold temperature. While various technical and financial problems ensured the project never came to fruition, it did demonstrate Churchill's willingness to envisage the future rather than simply waiting for it to arrive.

But Churchill's most significant reading of a situation

had nothing to do with technical innovation. It was, in hindsight, his ability to grasp the nature of Hitler and his regime in the 1930s that carried most impact. While Hitler's rebuilding of the German nation was held up as an example to others and members of the British elite eagerly associated with him, Churchill warned of the grave consequences of giving him too much free reign. Refusing to abandon what he regarded as his duty to urge caution, he was characterized as either an antiquated buffoon or as a warmonger by his opponents.

He was neither. He was, though, prescient. As early as 1930, he is reported to have told the son of the former 'Iron Chancellor', Otto von Bismarck, that he was convinced that Hitler and his followers would 'seize the first available opportunity to resort to armed force'. In an article written in 1933 he predicted the organized massacres of Jews: 'There is a danger of the odious conditions now ruling in Germany, being extended by conquest to Poland and another persecution and pogrom of Jews being begun in this new area.' In 1936, he laid out the future of the continent as he saw it:

> Europe is approaching a climax … Either there will be a melting of hearts and a joining of hands between great nations … or there will be an explosion and a catastrophe the course of which no imagination can measure, and beyond which no human eye can see.

He could hardly have made his case more strongly, but

still there was a powerful lobby that refused to accept his gloomy predictions.

His frustration grew as the government kicked its heels over rearmament for economic reasons. It was true that Churchill as Chancellor had been instrumental in tightening the defence budget, a fact his opponents used as a stick with which to beat him. But that was a decade ago, and now he saw that the sands had shifted. With Germany's military force growing, Churchill feared that Britain would be at a disadvantage in a conflict. Equally, he believed that 'an accumulation of deterrents against the aggressor' offered the best hope of avoiding war altogether.

By the time Prime Minister Neville Chamberlain arrived home from the Munich Conference in 1938, proclaiming 'peace in our time' in return for a portion of Czechoslovakian territory ceded to Berlin, Churchill's patience was used up. Responding to the Munich Agreement in October that year, he declaimed:

> The utmost my Rt. Hon. Friend the prime minister has been able to secure by his immense exertions ... the utmost he has been able to gain for Czechoslovakia in the matters which were in dispute has been that the German dictator, instead of snatching the victuals from the table, has been content to have them served to him course by course ... And do not suppose that this is the end. This is only the beginning of the reckoning.

How sadly accurate he turned out to be.

## See Which Way the Wind is Blowing

With any hope long gone of establishing a tactical advantage over Hitler by employing a little foresight, Churchill was brought back into the political spotlight in 1940 as prime minister. Had he been listened to earlier, his wartime tenure may have been a much easier one. Ironically, while he had read the international situation so accurately in the 1930s, he alas failed in his efforts to get others to see the world as he did until it was almost too late.

### LISTEN TO THE PEOPLE

There were points over Churchill's lifetime when he misread situations, too. His 'Gestapo speech' ahead of the 1945 election, for instance, was ill-judged and did not pay heed to the public mood. One of his least successful orations, he caused significant offence by claiming that a socialist government would impose rule via a political police force that he described as 'some form of Gestapo'. Many of these same 'socialists' were esteemed members of his wartime coalition who had worked hard to secure the public's trust. Having done wonders as wartime leader, he was not able to click into the electorate's domestic hopes for peacetime – a situation no doubt exacerbated by his continuing focus on securing an acceptable international post-war settlement.

Nonetheless, his ability to analyse complex situations on the international stage continued in the post-war period. His 'Iron Curtain' speech, for instance, envisaged the Cold War impasse that dominated global politics for the next forty-plus years. Meanwhile, back in 1924, he had written in *Pall Mall* magazine about the threat posed by the development of an atomic bomb:

> Mankind has never been in this position before. Without having improved appreciably in virtue or enjoying wiser guidance, it has got into its hands for the first time the tools by which it can unfailingly accomplish its own extermination … May there not be methods of using explosive energy incomparably more intense than anything heretofore discovered? Might not a bomb no bigger than an orange be found to possess a secret power to destroy a whole block of buildings – nay, to concentrate the force of a thousand tons of cordite and blast a township at a stroke?

Even Einstein was not overly angst-ridden about the prospect of nuclear war at that stage, so this was arguably Churchill at his most gloomily visionary.

As post-war Leader of the Opposition and then prime minister, Churchill fixed his gaze on the big international questions. There are those who felt this came at the expense of domestic concerns, but there is no denying that he grasped early issues that would come to dominate global politics for the remainder of the century and beyond. From communist tyranny and the threat of mutual annihilation to questions of collective security and European union, he had his finger well and truly on the pulse.

In the final reckoning, when it most mattered, there were few who comprehended Europe's reality in the 1930s as comprehensively and as readily as he.

# Hope for the Best and Prepare for the Worst

'When every step is fraught with grave
consequences and with real peril to the cause,
deliberate and measured action is not
merely prudent, but decent.'

WINSTON CHURCHILL IN A SPEECH TO
THE HOUSE OF COMMONS, 1910

Churchill might not have been much of a fan of Latin at school, but there was at least one phrase from the language that resonated with him: 'Si vis pacem, para bellum.' Translated, it reads 'If you desire peace, prepare for war.'

In the 1930s, there were times when he seemed to serve as the nation's harbinger of doom, but his utterances on Britain's unpreparedness for war were driven by a desire to jolt the government into addressing the country's shortcomings. As he put it in an address at the Carlton Club on 29 June 1939: 'There are two supreme obligations which rest upon a British government. They are of equal importance. One is to strive to prevent a war, and the other is to be ready if war should come.'

This single statement is key to understanding his determination to make known the threat of Hitler even at personal cost to himself. His critics always accused him of having had rather too much of a taste for war. It is true that the 'adventure' of war appealed to him on some level – he was someone who, as a boy, had sated himself on tales of great British military adventurers from earlier eras (including his own ancestors) and who had tasted front-line action himself.

However, it is wrong to suggest that war did not appal him in equal measure. In 1909 he had been present at the scene of German military manoeuvres and subsequently wrote the following to Clemmie: 'Much as war attracts me and fascinates my mind with its tremendous situations, I feel more deeply every year – and can measure the feeling here in the midst of arms – what vile and wicked folly and barbarism it all is.' This was a theme he returned to in 1930, when he wrote: 'War, which used to be cruel and magnificent, has now become cruel and squalid.'

But he was a realist, too. His wide reading of international history left him in no doubt that war was a tragic but natural part of the world order. In 1929, for instance, he observed in *The World Crisis*:

The story of the human race is war. Except for brief and precarious interludes there has never been peace in the world; and before history began, murderous strife was universal and unending. But the modern developments surely require severe and active attention.

It was this absence of 'active attention' that so disappointed him, particularly as he understood that once war was in progress, you put yourself into the hands of fate. Reflecting on a victory in the Battle of Britain that he knew so easily could have been a defeat, he commented at Chequers: 'What a slender thread the greatest of things can hang by.' Later on, in his *Second World War*, he described war as 'mainly a catalogue of blunders'. What he really meant was that it was pointless to believe you could control a war once you were in it.

However, he did believe that you stood the greatest chance of success if you had prepared properly in the relative benevolence of peacetime. Alas, that was something Britain had failed to do since the end of the Great War. 'We were so glutted with victory that in our folly we threw it away,' he ruefully suggested. Such complacency had been a failing of successive governments, and in 1938 he launched a particularly ferocious attack in Parliament on the record of the Chamberlain administration:

> They neither prevented Germany from rearming, nor did they rearm themselves in time. They quarrelled with Italy without saving Ethiopia. They exploited and discredited the vast institution of the League of Nations and they neglected to make alliances and combinations which might have repaired previous errors, and thus they left us in the hour of trial without adequate national defence or effective international security.

If Churchill did have a taste for battle in his youth, it is difficult to accuse him of the same in the lead-up to the Second World War. He could have done no more to try to avert conflict. His calls for rearmament were made in the belief that the mere presence of well-equipped armed forces would ensure they did not need to be put into action. That said, when war arrived he had the stomach for it. It was his conviction that once inevitable, war should be pursued energetically and proactively in order to overcome the enemy as quickly as possible. He had held similar views in the First World War, as when he told the House of Commons in 1916: 'We cannot go on treating the war as if it were an emergency which can be met by makeshifts. It is, until it is ended, the one vast, all-embracing industry of the nation, and it is until it is ended the sole aim and purpose of all our lives.'

Churchill had made himself a thorn in the side of the government in the 1930s with the aim that war might be put off. The governments of that decade buried their heads in the sand in the hope that war would not find them. When it did, they were not ready for it.

In 1942, Churchill spoke to the Boy Scouts Association, highly praising their founder, Robert Baden-Powell. It was no surprise that Churchill so admired a man who embodied the ethos 'Be prepared'.

## CHURCHILL AND HITLER

'This evil man, this monstrous abortion of hatred and defeat ...'

WINSTON CHURCHILL REFERRING TO ADOLF HITLER, 21 OCTOBER 1940

Hitler and Churchill never met, but Churchill had an instinctive sense of the man who would be his nemesis. 'I hate nobody except Hitler – and that is professional,' he would tell his private secretary, John Colville, in 1940.

It was unfortunate that Hitler's rise in Germany should so neatly coincide with Churchill's relative (and temporary) demise in Britain. Had Churchill been accepted into the bosom of government in the early 1930s, his foreboding regarding Germany might have found wider acceptance earlier.

Like many others within the ranks of British society, Churchill could see that Hitler had helped restore Germany's economy and sense of self in the aftermath of the First World War. In a now notorious speech of 1938, Churchill stated: 'I have always said that if Great Britain were defeated in war I hoped we should find a Hitler to lead us back to our rightful position among nations.' It is a speech that has often been construed as his praising the German leader. Churchill was suggesting that, instead, here was a man who could have achieved much but had so miserably failed to capitalize on his attributes.

But Churchill, quite rightly, did not fall into the trap of underestimating his opponent. Hitler was a skilled political operator (if an erratic military strategist) and to treat him as an incompetent would have been folly. Churchill realized that he did not have to like his enemies to be able to appreciate their abilities. During his time in South Africa at the turn of the century, for instance, he developed a grudging regard for the military skills of the Boers. Erwin Rommel, the 'Desert Fox' who commanded Hitler's forces in North Africa, was another who earned his reluctant respect. Reflecting in his *Second World War*, Churchill described Rommel as a 'splendid military gambler', writing:

His ardour and daring inflicted grievous disasters upon us, but he deserves the salute which I made him – and not without some reproaches from the public – in the House of Commons in January 1942, when I said of him, 'We have a very daring and skillful opponent against us, and, may I say across the havoc of war, a great general.' He also deserves our respect because, although a loyal German soldier, he came to hate Hitler and all his works, and took part in the conspiracy to rescue Germany by displacing the maniac and tyrant.

Similarly, Churchill respected aspects of Mussolini's leadership in Italy (he once referred to him as the 'greatest law-giver among living men' in an address to a meeting of anti-socialists and anti-communists in London in 1933), without buying into his wider political philosophy.

But to suggest that Churchill ever wavered in his repugnance of his opposite numbers in either Germany or Italy is a gross misrepresentation. He developed a particularly strong line in put-downs for Hitler, referring to him dismissively as 'Corporal Hitler' in reference to his rank within the Austrian army during the First World

War. And on a visit to France in 1945, Churchill even signed a shell destined for Berlin with the words 'Hitler, Personally'.

---

### OLD HATREDS DIE HARD

Churchill felt that the German population, which had voted Hitler into power, should take its share of the blame. Despite wishing to avoid besmirching the whole nation ('I have no prejudice against the German people,' he insisted in 1935), he was scathing in his criticisms. As early as 1930, his views were clear, writing in the *Strand Magazine*: '… in spite of all their brains and courage, they [the Germans] worship Power, and let themselves be led by the nose.' Three years later he described them as the 'most formidable people in the world' but 'now the most dangerous, a people who inculcate a form of blood-lust in their children, and lay down the doctrine that every frontier must be the starting point for invasion.'

---

His attitude to Hitler's regime is neatly summarized in the following passage from a speech he made in Parliament in October 1938:

There can never be friendship between the British democracy and the Nazi power, that power which spurns Christian ethics, which cheers its onward course by a barbarous paganism, which vaunts the spirit of aggression and conquest, which derives strength and perverted pleasure from persecution, and uses, as we have seen, with pitiless brutality the threat of murderous force. That power cannot ever be the trusted friend of the British democracy.

Yet even Churchill was shocked at the extent of the evil perpetrated by the Nazi machine. In common with the rest of the world, there was a sense of disbelief as evidence of the extent of the Holocaust came to light. When Churchill wrote to his Foreign Minister, Anthony Eden, in 1944, his disgust and outrage was evident:

There is no doubt that this is probably the greatest and most horrible crime ever committed in the whole history of the world, and it has been done by scientific machinery by nominally civilized men in the name of a great State and one of the leading races of Europe.

Churchill strongly advocated that all involved in the crimes, including those only following orders, should be executed after a trial. He also suggested making public declarations, so that everyone associated with the Holocaust was hunted down.

The characterization of the Führer as 'Corporal Hitler' served to undermine the enemy in wartime. But in the post-war period, such mimicry seemed almost distasteful and certainly inadequate. As Churchill wrote in *The Second World War*: 'Crimes were committed by the Germans under the Hitlerite domination ... which find no equal in scale and wickedness with any that have darkened the human record ...'

Churchill and Hitler were united in a profound love of their countries and shared a belief that their respective nations had earned the right to wield power and to be treated with respect. Both, too, believed in the entitlement to rule over a large empire, using force when necessary. Both, then, were ardent nationalists, but where Churchill championed democracy and personal liberty, Hitler advocated authoritarianism and suppressed all opposition. So how did they end up on opposite sides of the same coin? In May 1946, Churchill spoke at the States-General of the Netherlands on the subject of nationalism. His words serve to illustrate their fundamental difference. 'Where it [nationalism] means love of country and readiness to die for country; where it means love of tradition and culture and the gradual building up across the centuries of a social entity dignified by nationhood, then it is the first of virtues,' he said. 'Where nationalism means the lust for pride and power, the craze for supreme domination by weight or force; where it is the senseless urge to be the biggest in the world, it is a danger and a vice.'

'He is the most bloodthirsty or amateurish strategist in history … For over five years this man has been chasing around Europe like a madman in search of something that he could set on fire … His abnormal state of mind can only be explained as symptomatic either of a paralytic disease or of a drunkard's ravings.'

**ADOLF HITLER ON CHURCHILL, MAY 1941**

# Bounce Back
# with Grace

'As one's fortunes are reduced, one's spirit
must expand to fill the void.'

WINSTON CHURCHILL IN A LETTER TO HIS
WIFE DURING THE FIRST WORLD WAR

There have been few political rebirths as extraordinary as Churchill's in the Second World War. Having spent more than a decade virtually on the political scrapheap, he was parachuted into the most important job in the land at the most crucial time in the country's history. It must have been very tempting to gloat, but instead he demonstrated great dignity in assuming the premiership and approached his task with the gravitas it required.

Had the young Churchill found himself in that situation, his attitude might have been different. There is every prospect that a youthful incarnation would not have operated with the same decorum as the more seasoned version. He did, after all, have a reputation for getting carried away on the tide of events. One need only think of the Sidney Street Siege in 1911 or the defence of Antwerp in 1914. And come the 1926 General Strike, he was unable to subdue the journalistic demon within when the opportunity arose to take charge of the *British Gazette*. Operating out of the offices of the *Morning Post* (an erstwhile employer of his), he used the *Gazette* to trumpet some fairly crude government propaganda as he fought back against what he regarded as an outbreak of entirely unacceptable social disorder. In a typically belligerent editorial, for instance, he proclaimed: 'Either the country will break the general strike, or the general strike will break the country.'

However, by the time he found his way into Number 10, Churchill had experienced enough professional and personal reversals that he assumed the mantle with grace rather than bombast and arrogance. As the quote at the start of this section suggests, Churchill was often at his best in adversity. And he came to the premiership with year after year of adversity behind him, not to mention a few more in front of him.

If the Dardanelles affair of 1915 haunted his career, Churchill himself considered his biggest professional mistake to be the reintroduction of the Gold Standard, which set the value of the pound sterling in 1925. While his instinct was to consign the Gold Standard to history, he re-implemented it on the best advice of the economists of the day. The results included falling exports, deflation and mass unemployment, prompting the General Strike. Perhaps his frustration at that civil action was in part because he knew his own actions had helped cause it.

Once out of office in 1929, he suffered his 'wilderness years', during which enemies derided him and old allies all too often withheld their support. He was, to some extent, paying the price for past offences – both real and perceived. There were plenty of people within the

Conservative Party who had never forgiven him for joining the Liberals in 1904. Others were paying him back for championing free trade, for overseeing the Dardanelles episode, for his role in establishing Irish Home Rule and for bringing back the Gold Standard. When it really mattered, argued his critics, Winston's judgement was questionable.

When he spent the 1930s calling for expensive rearmament and solid opposition to German expansionism, he was accused of fomenting war. Then when it became obvious that Hitler could not be appeased, he found himself suddenly back in favour. Winston, that grand old man of British politics, had been right all along and, though there were rivals to take over the premiership, in the end there was no serious attempt to install anyone else.

Aware how quickly one's fortunes could change, he accepted his appointment to the post of prime minister with consummate humility. Churchill was a man who would experience at least six electoral defeats in his life – quite a record of failure for a figure so widely loved and praised. Then there were the vagaries of personal misfortune he had endured, from the death of an infant daughter to significant financial losses as a result of the 1929 Wall Street Crash. No wonder he learned to accept his triumphs in the same way as he contended with his trials – with considered circumspection.

Sure enough, there were more downturns in fortune to come, even for Britain's wartime saviour. King

George VI considered Churchill's defeat at the 1945 election as 'most ungrateful to you personally after all your hard work for the people'. Churchill, wounded by the electoral snub, could nonetheless make light of it. Amid talk of him receiving one of the land's highest honours, he reportedly queried: 'How can I accept the Order of the Garter, when the people of England have just given me the Order of the Boot?' By then in his seventies, he responded to that setback in his inimitable style: by winning the next general election and returning to Downing Street.

'If' by Rudyard Kipling, whose writings Churchill so admired, contains a sentiment to which Churchill came to subscribe:

If you can meet with Triumph and Disaster
And treat those two impostors just the same;
… Yours is the Earth and everything that's in it,
And – which is more – you'll be a Man, my son.

## MOVING INTO NUMBER 10

'I have nothing to offer but blood,
toil, tears and sweat.'

WINSTON CHURCHILL IN HIS FIRST SPEECH AS
PRIME MINISTER, 13 MAY 1940

Churchill in his time held three of the four great offices of state: Chancellor of the Exchequer, Home Secretary and prime minister. Only the office of Foreign Secretary eluded him in completing the set. His entry into 10 Downing Street on 10 May 1940 was greeted by cheering crowds. Always a man for the big stage, he took to his new role with gusto from the outset.

Things had moved quickly. On 7 May, Neville Chamberlain had won a vote of confidence in the House of Commons following a debate on Britain's flawed campaign against German forces in Norway. Despite his technical victory in the poll, Chamberlain knew his time was up. He, Lord Halifax and Churchill held secret discussions as to who should succeed him. Chamberlain favoured Halifax, as did many of the Conservative Party members. So too did the king, George VI, though in time he came to value Churchill greatly. But for reasons still not entirely clear, Halifax stood aside and Churchill stepped in. In retrospect, it was doubtless the right decision: since Halifax was so closely associated with the government's appeasement policy, Labour's leadership had made it clear they did not wish to serve under him, and it is questionable whether he really desired the top job anyway.

Churchill gave his first speech to the Commons as premier on 13 May. It proved to be one of the defining orations of his career.

I would say to the House, as I said to those who have joined this government: 'I have nothing to offer but blood, toil, tears and sweat.' We have before us an ordeal of the most grievous kind. We have before us many, many long months of struggle and of suffering. You ask, what is our policy? I can say: It is to wage war, by sea, land and air, with all our might and with all the strength that God can give us; to wage war against a monstrous tyranny, never surpassed in the dark, lamentable catalogue of human crime. That is our policy. You ask, what is our aim? I can answer in one word: It is victory, victory at all costs, victory in spite of all terror, victory, however long and hard the road may be; for without victory, there is no survival. Let that be realized; no survival for the British Empire, no survival for all that the British Empire has stood for, no survival for the urge and impulse of the ages, that mankind will move forward towards its goal. But I take up my task with buoyancy and hope ...

So began the process of steeling the nation for the challenges ahead. The 'blood, toil, tears and sweat' image was such a potent one that he used the phrase in no less than six speeches between his assuming office and the end of 1942.

Churchill considered that this was what fate had always intended for him. Looking back on his first night in the role, he reported feeling a profound sense of relief, and that his destiny had finally claimed him, his past life being but a preparation for the trial. He was not, though, blind to the scale of the challenge that lay before him. As he was greeted by an adoring public, he confided to General Ismay (his chief military advisor): 'Poor people, poor people. They trust me, and I can give them nothing but disaster for quite a long time.'

That did not prove quite the case. Though there was little to celebrate in his first months and even years in office, outright disaster was averted. Had the Battle of Britain been lost in 1940, for instance, or the British forces destroyed at Dunkirk, the nation's prospects would have been very bleak. As it was, each successive challenge was overcome, each setback absorbed, until in late 1942 Churchill was able to tentatively talk of the 'end of the beginning' of the war. Under his leadership, the country enjoyed a palpable upturn in fortunes that would have been all but unimaginable under the continuing tenure of Chamberlain or a divided government led by Lord Halifax.

# Lead from the Front

'There is only one duty, only one safe course,
and that is to try to be right and not fear to do or
say what you believe to be right. That is the only
way to deserve and to win the confidence of
our great people in these days of trouble.'

**WINSTON CHURCHILL IN A SPEECH TO
THE HOUSE OF COMMONS, 1941**

Churchill could not be described as a shrinking violet. He felt that he was born to lead, although he surely could never have predicted just where destiny would take him. However, there is a vast chasm between believing one is destined for a job and having the skills necessary to execute the role well. The famous historian A. J. P. Taylor described Churchill in his much-respected *English History 1914-1945* as 'the saviour of his country'. So what attributes, honed over a lifetime, did Churchill bring to the job?

As we have already discussed, Churchill was a masterful reader of situations. He was, too, a very accomplished strategist, both politically and militarily. He made his mistakes on both counts (for instance, his stance on the Gold Standard and, arguably, his devotion to the Gallipoli misadventure) but tended to learn from his errors. He had, let it also be remembered, personally taken part in military expeditions on no less than four continents.

Among his greatest strengths was consistency. During the war, when everyday life was turned upside down, he emerged as a touchstone of constancy – the determined, nerveless, cigar-chewing John Bull on whom the country could depend. Yet he was able to combine these characteristics with notable flexibility, too. He prided himself on his willingness to change tack when he had been convinced it was the right thing to do. One of his favourite maxims was: 'I would rather be right than consistent.' On another occasion he said, 'In the course of my life I have often had to eat my words, and I must confess that I have always found it a wholesome diet.'

His wartime coalition was truly inclusive. He outlined his take on 'national unity' in a speech in the Commons in August 1939: 'It surely means that reasonable sacrifices of party opinions, personal opinion, and party interest should be made by all in order to contribute to the national security.' Furthermore, he put faith in the opinions of his military chiefs of staff and resisted the temptation to pull rank or overrule them. For an individual invested with so much personal authority, he rarely fell victim to hubris.

Yet in general, once he had decided on a course of action, he stuck to it. Amid the instability of war, that proved a great reassurance to people. In a speech he had made all the way back in 1929, he had emphasized the importance of avoiding 'chops and changes of policy'. He also found the indeterminacy of the Chamberlain administration particularly enraging as when, in 1936, he addressed Parliament thus:

The government simply cannot make up their minds, or they cannot get the prime minister to make up his mind. So they go on in strange paradox, decided only to be undecided, resolved to be irresolute, adamant for drift, solid for fluidity, all-powerful to be impotent. So we go on preparing more months and years – precious, perhaps vital to the greatness of Britain – for the locusts to eat.

Churchill was publicly humble about his role. He described how the people of the nation were a lion and that it had fallen to him merely to provide the roar. But in the day-to-day execution of his premiership he was highly demanding. He kept to an unusual timetable that customarily involved working in bed until lunchtime, followed by daytime naps and periods of frenetic activity long into the night. He would often dictate speeches, missives and ideas from his bath and he upset more secretaries than the average employment tribunal could cope with. But for all that, he inspired extraordinary loyalty from the vast majority of his staff.

Few could fail to marvel at the volume of work he got through, or his ability to analyse great wads of paperwork to get to the core of an issue. He was blessed with a strong work ethic and demanded those around him to keep pace. Even the general public were expected to keep their noses to the grindstone. In broadcast after broadcast he implored the ordinary people of the country to put up with their hardships and, in essence, to KBO. Consider his famous 'finest hour' address to the House of Commons in 1940, in which he prepared the public for the forthcoming Battle of Britain: 'Let us therefore brace ourselves to our duties, and so bear ourselves that, if the British Empire and its Commonwealth last for a thousand years, men will still say, "This was their finest hour."'

Just as he did not shirk hard work, nor did he shrink from taking personal responsibility. The buck stopped with him and he bore the onerous burden with fortitude. His reflections on the Dardanelles campaign in the First World War provide a clear insight into his attitude:

Nobody ever launched an attack without having misgivings beforehand. You ought to have misgivings before; but when the moment of action is come, the hour of misgivings is passed. It is often not possible to go backward from a course which has been adopted in war. A man must answer 'Aye' or 'No' to the great questions which are put, and by that decision he must be bound.

In short, Churchill realized that successful leadership combines fortitude and dependability along with a willingness to recognize and mine the talents of others.

# It's the Way You Say It

'There is nothing that gives greater pleasure to a
speaker than seeing his great points go home.'

WINSTON CHURCHILL IN A SPEECH, 1927

Churchill's qualities as a leader were many and varied, but would he be remembered in such high esteem if he hadn't bequeathed us a body of oratory that is nearly unmatched in history? Almost certainly not. That he lived in an age where significant numbers of his speeches were recorded has no doubt helped consolidate his legend.

Rhetoric – the art of effective or persuasive speaking or writing – was highly prized in the classical world. In today's era of professional spin doctors and cynical news agendas, it can seem like a less noble skill. Churchill, though, never underestimated the power of great communication. Nor did his oratorical output rely on a supporting army of 'for hire' speech-writers. In 1896 he told Bourke Cockran, a New York politician and an unofficial mentor to the young Churchill:

From what I have seen, I know that there are few more fascinating experiences than to watch a great mass of people under the wand of the magician. There is no gift so rare or so precious as the gift of oratory [that is] so difficult to define or impossible to acquire.

Churchill's style of delivery evolved in response to his various speech impediments. His maiden speech in the Commons in 1901 was broadly well received, although some newspapers referred to his 'unfortunate lisp'. Other commentators would pick up on a slightly grating tone to his voice in the early years, and a delivery that could be hesitant and flat. These were issues he consciously addressed as time passed, setting a precedent for the likes of Margaret Thatcher who remodelled her own vocal patterns in the interests of her career. Churchill evolved a style that was hardly flamboyant. Instead he learned speeches as if they were scripts and perfected a slowish-paced delivery that capitalized on his deep tones. His vocal ticks became not distracting impediments but characterful quirks.

He was also a masterful creator of content. By ruthless editing of his words, he was able to make his case with clarity and authority. He also had the ability to keep his audience interested, something that was never more vital than in wartime.

So what rules make for a great Churchill oration?
• Focus on a single theme at a time. Churchill realized that there was no point in bombarding his audience with complex arguments that would lose their attention. In 1919, for instance, he told the Prince of Wales (later Edward VIII): 'If you have an important point to make, don't try to be subtle or clever. Use a piledriver. Hit the point once. Then come back and hit it again. Then hit it a third time.'

## It's the Way You Say It

- Use simple language. It is tempting to demonstrate one's mastery of language, and Churchill certainly was a master. Yet he realized that powerful messages are best communicated by accessible language. No one wants to listen to a show-off!
- Don't sugar-coat. War brings hardships and Churchill was convinced that the British people could deal with whatever was thrown at them as long as their leaders were honest with them. As he told the House of Commons in 1941: 'They [the British] are the only people who like to be told how bad things are, who like to be told the worst.'
- Offer hope. While honesty is the best policy, give people optimism that things will get better.
- Add colour. Churchill employed a number of methods to keep his speeches interesting, from creating gripping narratives and memorable imagery to invoking history and expressing profound emotion.
- Inspire. Churchill's speeches were designed to unite people around him. Give them a reason to join your team!

Churchill was unsurpassed in his ability to say just the right thing at the right time. Looking back over his many decades as a public figure, it is possible to pick out standout speeches in virtually every phase of his career. But if forced to choose one period of speechmaking as his greatest, it is difficult to look beyond 1940 when he took over as prime minister with the UK facing the real prospect of being invaded by German forces. In a series of epoch-defining addresses, he immortalized countless phrases and idioms that still rattle off the tongue today.

He started with the 'blood, toil, tears and sweat' speech that so galvanized the public and a few weeks later was famously priming them to carry the fight to Hitler even as large tracts of Europe fell. 'We shall go on to the end,' he said. 'We shall fight in France, we shall fight on the seas and oceans, we shall fight with growing confidence and growing strength in the air, we shall defend our island, whatever the cost may be, we shall fight on the beaches, we shall fight on the landing grounds, we shall fight in the fields and in the streets, we shall fight in the hills; we shall never surrender ...'

With the Battle of Britain looming in June 1940 (upon which 'depends the survival of Christian civilization ... our own British life, and the long continuity of our institutions and our Empire'), he continued to deliver inspiration in spades. 'Let us therefore brace ourselves to our duties,' he implored, 'and so bear ourselves that, if the British Empire and its Commonwealth last for a thousand years, men will still say, "This was their finest hour."' When it was all over, he led the plaudits for the British airmen with the immortal line: 'Never in the field of human conflict was so much owed by so many to so few.' These few short examples give but a tiny taste of his output at this time and serve to show how he created a national narrative through sumptuous use of language.

> 'He mobilized the English language
> and sent it into battle.'
> JOHN F. KENNEDY, ON THE OCCASION OF
> GRANTING CHURCHILL HONORARY US
> CITIZENSHIP IN 1963

Given his love of English and his impatience at its abuse, it is therefore surprising that he had a dalliance with a form of the language called Basic English. Comprising fewer than a thousand words, it was the brainchild of linguist Charles Kay Ogden in 1930. The idea was that this cut-down form of the language could be used internationally and assist the learning of English as a second tongue. In a speech in 1943 Churchill said: 'I am very much interested in the question of Basic English. The widespread use of this would be a gain for us far more durable and fruitful than the annexation of great provinces. It would also fit in with my ideas of closer union with the United States by making it even more worthwhile to belong to the English-speaking club.'

F. D. Roosevelt, the American president, was less keen, writing to Churchill in June 1944 with the following observations: 'I wonder what the course of history would have been, if in May 1940 you had been able to offer the British people only "blood, work, eye water, and face water", which I understand is the best Basic English can do with five famous words.'

Despite that ill-advised flirtation with Basic English, today there is no greater honour for a public speaker than to have an address described as Churchillian.

# Maintain a Sense of Humour

'All babies look like me. But then,
I look like all babies.'

WINSTON CHURCHILL ON BEING TOLD
BY A FRIEND THAT THEIR GRANDCHILD
RESEMBLED HIM

As first a soldier and then a politician, Churchill pursued careers not particularly known for their light-heartedness. He held senior offices through the dark days of two world wars, was at the forefront of public life as the country lurched into economic crisis and lived an existence that demanded metaphorical firefighting almost continuously. Yet through it all, he retained a reputation for humour and loved nothing better than to deliver a well-placed bon mot.

As the quotation on the previous page suggests, much of his humour was self-deprecating. Churchill's ego was not so great that he could not recognize his own foibles and frailties. In addition, he had a good understanding of how others saw him. He also, predictably, adored wordplay. In an interview with the *Morning Post* in 1902, for instance, he responded to a question about the life of a politician with the comment: 'He is asked to stand, he wants to sit and he is expected to lie …' On another occasion, legend has it, President Roosevelt came to see Churchill in his private rooms, only to be greeted by the premier completely nude as he emerged from his bath.

'You see,' Churchill is reputed to have said, 'the British prime minister has nothing to hide from the president of the United States.' If only all international negotiations could be undertaken in such a spirit of transparency.

However, Churchill was not one to limit his jokes only to those at his own expense. He was a caustic wit who was not above savaging those who crossed him. Can there be a more cutting assessment of an opponent than his observation that Clement Atlee, the Labour prime minister who defeated him at the polls in 1945, had 'much to be modest about'. Meanwhile, his pursuit of a winning line could sometimes lead to unfortunate lapses in gallantry. One of the first female MPs, Bessie Braddock, is said to have accused him one day of being 'disgustingly drunk'. Rapier-sharp, but rather uncharitably, he responded: 'Bessie, my dear, you are ugly, and what's more, you are disgustingly ugly. But tomorrow I shall be sober and you will still be disgustingly ugly.'

There has long been debate as to whether this incident really happened, but the latest evidence suggests that it did, although he lifted the sentiment of his response (if not the exact wording) from the comic film star, W. C. Fields. Churchill had an unfortunate habit of upsetting female Members of Parliament, with Nancy Astor another to fall out with him. 'Winston, if I were married to you, I'd put poison in your coffee,' she told him one day. 'Nancy, if I were married to you, I'd drink it,' he retorted.

Then there were the times when he directed his comic

eye at officialdom. Generally enraged by bureaucratic doublespeak, he responded badly one day in 1944 to a civil service memo objecting to a sentence that finished with a preposition. Proving that the pen can indeed be mightier than the sword, he cut down the petty official by adding a note in the margin: 'This is the kind of tedious nonsense up with which I will not put!' There was a war to be won after all ...

## CHURCHILL AND THE BLACK DOG

'I have got a black dog on my back today.'

AN EXPRESSION CHURCHILL
USED ON SEVERAL OCCASIONS

That Churchill was able to see the lighter side of life was an undoubted blessing. Due to the seriousness of much of his life's work, it was perhaps essential, especially given that he was prone to darker mood swings too.

Churchill famously referred to the gloom that sporadically descended upon him as the 'black dog', although it was not a phrase he originated. Samuel Johnson must take credit for that and it was certainly a term in fairly wide usage during the Victorian age in which Churchill grew up. But how serious were these fits of gloom? It is a question that has fascinated scholars for decades now, and the jury remains defiantly out.

The debate centres around one key issue: did Churchill suffer significant, clinical depression or did he simply endure the same mood swings to which virtually everyone is prone at one time or another? Given the roller-coaster nature of his life and the weightiness of the issues that he had to deal with (can there be anything graver than to send thousands of people into war?), it would hardly be a surprise if melancholia sometimes overtook him. His father, too, suffered fits of deep sadness and one of Winston's daughters would take her own life – evidence, perhaps, of a family frailty.

There are those today (sometimes with their own agendas to promote) who depict Churchill as a manic-depressive. He has become in some quarters a poster boy for how mental disorder may be overcome. It has even been suggested that Churchill's early distrust of Hitler when others continued to praise him was the result of Churchill's peculiarly dark view of the world. But there is precious little clinical evidence to support these representations.

Nonetheless, Churchill considered his dark moods a significant problem. Why else would he give them a name? His worst episode seems to have occurred around the early 1910s, in his radical Liberal days. In later life he would tell his doctor: 'For two or three years the light faded from the picture. I sat in the House of Commons, but black depression settled on me.' He went on to confide: 'I don't like standing near the edge of the platform when an express train is passing through.'

Clementine, however, was less convinced that there was a serious problem. She acknowledged that he was sometimes depressed, but felt it was no different to that which most people experience, never being particularly bad or lasting excessively long. On the other hand, Clementine was an exponent of the 'stiff upper lip', so perhaps she was not the best person to judge. Yet her opinions chime closely with the work of modern scholars such as Wilfred Attenborough, who argues that any mental disorder was less serious than often postulated but likely comprised a complex mix of symptoms.

However bad or lengthy his mood swings were, it does not seem they affected the carrying out of his public duties unduly, and many instances could arguably be excused, given the catalogue of crises with which he was confronted over the course of his career.

# Connect with the Common People

'We have a deep respect for public opinion but
we do not let our course be influenced from
day to day by Gallup Polls.'

WINSTON CHURCHILL IN A SPEECH
IN MARGATE, 1953

As the quote on the previous page implies, Churchill believed in proactive government. However, he never forgot that government was there to serve the people and that their goodwill and co-operation was required for it to function efficiently. This was never truer than in times of conflict. At the end of 1941, he spoke to the Canadian parliament in Ottawa, detailing how everyone had their role to play:

> In this strange, terrible world war there is a place for everyone, man and woman, old and young, hale and halt; service in a thousand forms is open. There is no room now for the dilettante, the weakling, for the shirker, or the sluggard … The enemies ranged against us, coalesced and combined against us, have asked for total war. Let us make sure they get it.

Despite the elevated status to which he was born, Churchill had an instinctive affinity with the common man – arguably, much more so than with those of his own class. As a writer and soldier, he was keen to mix with people from all social strata and, as we have seen, advocated some radical social policies in his early years in government with the Liberals – so much so that on occasion he was accused of being a traitor to his class.

Although his affection for the 'common man' could easily have come across as patronizing, given that Churchill faced few of their everyday problems, he was careful never to speak down to the public or blatantly to curry favour with them. Addressing the Commons in 1941, for example, he said:

If today I am very kindly treated by the mass of the people of this country, it is certainly not because I have followed public opinion in recent years. There is only one duty, only one safe course, and that is to try to be right and not to fear to do or to say what you believe to be right. That is the only way to deserve and to win the confidence of our great people in these days of trouble.

Nor, as previously mentioned, would he attempt to paint a bleak situation as better than it was. He was never afraid to treat the general public as grown-ups. In *The Second World War*, he wrote:

There is no worse mistake in public leadership than to hold out false hopes soon to be swept away. The British people can face peril or misfortune with fortitude and buoyancy, but they bitterly resent being deceived or finding that those responsible for their affairs are themselves dwelling in a fool's paradise.

He deeply admired the way the population at large dealt with the hardships of war. In 1941 he described going about the country and seeing the damage wrought by the enemy, but was heartened by the 'quiet, confident, bright and smiling eyes beaming with a consciousness of being associated with a cause far higher and wider than any human or personal issue … I see the spirit of an unconquerable people,' he concluded.

And when victory was at last secured, Churchill was quick to give praise to the country as a whole. Speaking from London on VE Day on 8 May 1945, he said:

This is your victory! It is the victory of the cause of freedom in every land. In all our long history we have never seen a greater day than this. Everyone, man or woman, has done their best. Everyone has tried. Neither the long years, nor the dangers, nor the fierce attacks of the enemy, have in any way weakened the unbending resolve of the British nation. God bless you all.

It is also worth noting that Churchill's entire parliamentary career took place in the Commons, with not a minute spent in the House of Lords. He was offered a dukedom by Queen Elizabeth II after the end of his second spell as prime minister (he might have become the Duke of London), but turned it down. There were assorted reasons, including a concern that his elevation to the Upper House might hinder the prospective political career of his son, Randolph. But whatever the motives, it was fitting that Churchill, high-born but with the common touch, should die as 'the great commoner'.

# Fight, Not Flight

'Men and kings must be judged in the testing
moments of their lives. Courage is rightly esteemed
the first of human qualities because, as has been
said, it is the quality which guarantees all others.'

WINSTON CHURCHILL, WRITING IN
THE *STRAND MAGAZINE*, 1931

As a wartime leader, perhaps Churchill's greatest achievement was to maintain the nation's appetite for the fight. Once his efforts to head off Hitler at the pass in the 1930s had come to nought and war was inevitable, he was fully committed to seeing it through. While the appeasement strategy of the Chamberlain administration diminished their moral authority and their ability to inspire the country after war was declared, Churchill faced no such problems.

It is worth repeating that Churchill did not take war lightly. The reality of fighting appalled him, as his reflections in *The World Crisis* on the First World War in 1916 show:

This war proceeds along its terrible path by the slaughter of infantry ... I say to myself every day. What is going on while we sit here, while we go away to dinner or home to bed? Nearly 1,000 – Englishmen, Britishers, men of our race – are knocked into bundles of bloody rags every twenty-four hours, and carried away to hasty graves or to field ambulances ...

Having seen the grim business of war up close, he was convinced that the quickest way to end a conflict was to commit to fighting wholeheartedly. In a speech on the Boer War in 1901, he had argued, 'Once you are so unfortunate as to be drawn into a war, no price is too great to pay for an early and victorious peace.' He was making the same argument in an official note (retained in *The Second World War*) forty-three years later:

At the present stage of the war in Europe our overall strategic concept should be the engagement of the enemy on the largest scale with the greatest violence and continuity. In this way only shall we bring about an early collapse. Here is the prime test.

Churchill was like a firewalker who knows that the best way to avoid burning your feet is to walk over the hot coals quickly and confidently. But communicating that message to a novice looking at the coals smouldering before them is quite a different matter. Yet time and again he succeeded in persuading the country to follow his lead. He stirred the public to keep up momentum after each success and revived flagging spirits after each setback. As he put it to one of his wartime secretaries, Elizabeth Nel, 'We must go on and on like the gun-horses, till we drop.' Was this talent to inspire one he alone had? It is impossible to say, though it might just be the case. It seems highly unlikely a Chamberlain or a Halifax or even an Atlee could have done the same.

'It was because he was a great human being that, in our darkest days, he lit the lamps of hope at many firesides and released so many from the chains of despair. There has been nobody like him in our lifetimes … There have been, in the course of recorded history, some men of power who have cast shadows across the world. Winston Churchill, on the contrary, was a fountain of light and of hope.'

ROBERT MENZIES, AUSTRALIAN PRIME MINISTER, 1965

In his desire to be honest with the public, he rarely played down the challenges that lay ahead. In his early days in office in 1940, for instance, he did not even rule out the prospect that Britain might yet succumb to the enemy. Speaking from Downing Street just a couple of weeks into his tenure, he proclaimed: 'If at last the long story is to end, it were better it should end, not through surrender, but only when we are rolling senseless on the ground.' That is an extraordinary sentiment for a modern wartime leader to communicate, yet it succeeded in being both realistic and inspirational.

In March 1940, he told his fellow MPs: 'We must be ready, as we have always been ready, to take the rough with the smooth.' Nor would he ever allow complacency to enter his discourse. The job in hand was an arduous one and no one was to get carried away until ultimate victory had been achieved. 'The road to victory may not be so long as we expect,' he said in August that year. 'But we have no right to count upon this. Be it long or short, rough or smooth, we mean to reach our journey's end.' That was the reason why even a landmark victory such as that achieved at El Alamein was celebrated in muted terms. It did not signify the end, he was quick to emphasize, or even the beginning of the end – merely the end of the beginning.

Once embroiled in a battle, Churchill could not countenance fleeing. The only option, as far as he was concerned, was to fight your way out of it. Having divined that Hitler was not a man with whom one could effectively employ diplomacy, he prepared himself for a grim struggle – one he understood would most likely be to the death. The time for passivity had long gone, a fact implicit in a phrase he used on repeated occasions throughout the Second World War: 'I never "worry" about action, but only about inaction.'

# Churchill's Dark Side

'Are we beasts? Are we taking things too far?'

CHURCHILL'S RESPONSE TO THE BLANKET
BOMBING OF GERMAN CITIES IN
THE SECOND WORLD WAR

For all the popular adulation Churchill received in the last twenty-five years of his life and even more so in death, there are plenty of commentators who have found his choices at different stages of his life wanting. He is variously accused of being a racist imperialist, a misogynist, thuggish in dealing with popular protest and ruthless in wartime.

Some of his critics are perhaps too ready to judge him by the moral standards of our own time. If a few of his ethical positions are discomforting today, he nonetheless held the vast majority of them in good faith. However, that said, it would be remiss to fail to acknowledge that he was a controversial figure even in his own era and that several of his attitudes, positions and actions were highly divisive. It would be, perhaps, a miracle if some of his conduct over an extraordinarily long career was not at least questionable.

With the power of hindsight, we can see that there were some errors in judgement – and some of those more serious than others. Indeed, he himself came to seriously revise his position on several key subjects, including the women's rights movement and India's independence leader, Mahatma Gandhi. Perhaps we ought to be glad that we do not have to face some of the often criticized decisions he had to face.

### THE BRITISH BULLDOG ATTACKS

Churchill undoubtedly had a streak of ruthlessness in him. Fiercely loyal to friends, allies and staff, he inspired similar loyalty from others. But if you crossed him, you would do so at your own peril. Some of his most savage personal attacks were upon those who had let him down. For example, when in 1941 a parliamentary select committee cited Bob Boothby (Churchill's old colleague and former parliamentary private secretary at the Treasury) for not declaring a financial interest while holding public office, the prime minister showed him little compassion. He suggested that Boothby ought to 'join a bomb disposal squad as the best way of rehabilitating himself in the eyes of his fellow men. After all, the bombs might not go off.'

Churchill could not abide civic disorder, regardless of how just a cause lay behind it. He believed that Britain's parliamentary democracy provided the appropriate political channels in which protest could be expressed.

Unscheduled and violent disorder, however, threatened to undermine the very fabric of the democratic system that he so loved. Take the 1926 General Strike. Churchill the Liberal reformer of a couple of decades earlier would no doubt have sympathized with the plight of the 'working man', many of whom had returned from the First World War only to find themselves living below the 'minimum standard'. But when workers across industries withdrew their labour and took their protests to the streets, seriously threatening the economy, Churchill virtually went on to a war footing against the Trades Union Congress coordinating the action. Under his stewardship, the *British Gazette* seemed intent only on stirring emotions and precipitating a conclusive confrontation. It was an episode in which cooler circumspection might have served him better, but Churchill could not bring himself to back down in the face of what he considered outrageous provocation.

If the General Strike brought out the scrapper in Churchill, so too did the Suffragette movement. Although not utterly opposed to their demands in principle, to the chagrin of Clementine, he grew increasingly sceptical of introducing votes for women. He was concerned about how a restructured electorate might alter the political landscape and was unconvinced that the majority of women wanted the vote anyway. As the Suffragette movement upped the ante with increasingly violent actions (Clemmie even had to fight off one woman who attempted to push her husband onto a railway line), his attitude only hardened and he repeatedly dismissed their cause at public meetings. Nor did his standing with them improve when, as Home Secretary, he refused to ban the controversial process of force-feeding Suffragette prisoners (although he did grant them 'political prisoner' status).

After the First World War, when women played such a vital role keeping the home front going, he became far more open to the prospect of female suffrage. By the time of the Second World War, which began eleven years after women were finally granted the same voting rights as men, he was far more gracious about their role. 'This war effort could not have been achieved if the women had not marched forward in millions and undertaken all kinds of tasks and work for which any other generation but our own ... would have considered them unfitted,' he told an audience at the Royal Albert Hall in September 1943. In the same speech, he pondered: 'It may seem strange that a great advance in the position of women in the world in industry, in controls of all kinds, should be made in time of war and not in time of peace ... War has taught us to make these vast strides forward towards a far more complete equalization of the parts to be played by men and women in society.' These were, though, belated and hard-earned concessions from a man who had done little to support female suffrage when its advocates pursued a course of moderately violent civil disorder.

Inevitably, Churchill's war record has been infinitely scrutinized and perhaps his single most controversial action between 1939 and 1945 was to grant permission for the blanket bombing of Dresden in February 1945. While there were legitimate military targets dotted around the urban expanse, its cultural hub and residential quarters were also devastated, with estimates of the death toll varying between 25,000 and 200,000. Only some ten per cent of Dresden was left standing by the end of the month.

Back in 1940, Churchill had spoken out against such bombing tactics. When an MP claimed the public hungered for an all-out campaign against German towns, Churchill chided:

> My dear Sir, this is a military and not a civilian war. You and others may desire to kill women and children. We desire (and have succeeded in our desire) to destroy German military objectives.

By 1942 his tone was changing, though. In a wireless broadcast in May that year, he set out how civilians might avoid being caught up in bombing raids on military targets:

> The civil population of Germany have, however, an easy way to escape from these severities. All they have to do is to leave the cities where munitions work is being carried on, abandon their work and go out into the fields and watch the home fires burning from a distance. In this way they may find time for

meditation and repentance. There they may remember the millions of Russian women and children they have driven out to perish in the snows and the mass executions of peasantry and prisoners of war which in varying scale they are inflicting upon so many of the ancient and famous peoples of Europe.

Certainly, the Dresden bombing came after severe provocation from Hitler, including the large-scale destruction of Rotterdam in the Netherlands and the English city of Coventry. Among the British military hierarchy, the policy was unofficially justified on the basis that it would destroy the German spirit and thus bring the war to an end at the earliest opportunity. The likes of Arthur 'Bomber' Harris, head of Bomber Command, argued strongly for the go-ahead. Churchill duly gave it, but by the following month was displaying serious reservations. He wrote a draft memo to the military Chiefs of Staff:

It seems to me that the moment has come when the question of bombing of German cities simply for the sake of increasing the terror, though under other pretexts, should be reviewed. Otherwise we shall come into control of an utterly ruined land ... The destruction of Dresden remains a serious query against the conduct of Allied bombing. I am of the opinion that military objectives must henceforward be more strictly studied in our own interests than that of the enemy.

Other German cities that had been earmarked for similar treatment were thus spared (to a degree at least). The terrible fate of Dresden, though, left deep scars in the psyches of both the Germans and the Allies. Whether it could be justified on strategic grounds remains highly contentious. Clearly Churchill had serious moral qualms about the action. Equally, though, it could not have happened without his agreement. Perhaps the lesson is that even if you are on the 'right side', war has a terrible habit of acquainting you with the darkest aspects of your soul.

## CHURCHILL AND THE EMPIRE

'Alone among the nations of the world we have found the means to combine empire and liberty.'

WINSTON CHURCHILL, 1940

A particularly controversial aspect of Churchill's character from our modern perspective was his attitude to empire. As previously discussed, he had been raised in the golden age of empire, when ideas that Britain was not only entitled to an empire but that its foreign subjects were lucky to have such enlightened rulers were commonly accepted. It was a powerful narrative to which much of the population across the classes subscribed. However, it is an argument that relies on a belief in inherent racial superiority that has little place in modern political discourse.

For instance, in his 1908 book *My African Journey*, Churchill reiterated the then popular notion of the 'noble savage', describing the 'African aboriginal' as 'secure in his abyss of contented degradation, rich in that he lacks everything and wants nothing'. Even more disconcerting was the evidence he gave to the Palestine Royal Commission in 1937 about the Arabs in Palestine:

I do not admit that the dog in the manger has the final right to the manger, even though he may have lain there for a very long time. I do not admit that right. I do not admit, for instance, that a great wrong has been done to the Red Indians of America, or the black people of Australia. I do not admit that a wrong has been done to those people by the fact that a stronger race, a higher-grade race, or, at any rate, a more worldly wise race, to put it that way, has come in and taken their place. I do not admit it. I do not think the Red Indians had any right to say, 'The American Continent belongs to us and we are not going to have any of these European settlers coming in here.'

Where indigenous uprisings threatened, he advocated a stern response. In 1919, he responded to a Kurdish rebellion in British-ruled Mesopotamia (modern-day Iraq) with a secret memorandum that read: 'I am strongly in favour of using poisoned gas against uncivilized tribes.' He went on to argue that gasses that 'cause great inconvenience and would spread a lively terror and yet would leave no serious permanent effects on most of those affected' were preferable to shells or bullets. However, this 'humanitarianism' cannot conceal the inherent principle of racial supremacy in the initial statement. Meanwhile, the conduct of British forces (including allegations of systematic torture) sent to crush the Mau Mau uprising in Kenya in 1952 remains a source of much controversy to this day. From the beginning of his career to its end, Churchill's desire to bolster the British Empire brought out in him a frequently brutal approach towards its foreign subjects.

As the jewel in the crown of the Empire, India was particularly prized by Churchill. So Gandhi, the key man in its quest for independence, came in for particular vitriol. Churchill's fundamental attitude to empire in general, and India in particular, is illuminated by a speech he made in Manchester in 1904:

But on what does our rule in India depend? It is not on terror, it is not on physical force, it is not on the superior knowledge of our government. I say that 30,000 civilians and 70,000 soldiers would be utterly insufficient to preserve our rule in India for a month if it were not known that our motives were pure and lofty, and that we sought the welfare of the Indian people. British justice is the foundation stone of British dominion.

Churchill continued to genuinely believe in the benevolence of British hegemony. As London prepared to relinquish control of India in 1947, he spoke in terms of 'abandonment' and described India as a territory 'over which we possess unimpeachable sovereignty'. He feared the state would 'fall into all the horrors of sanguinary civil war' (a fairly accurate assessment as it turned out) and believed the transfer of power was happening too rapidly.

Churchill was convinced he was showing compassion for the dominion. 'I have got real fears for the future,' he had told G. D. Birla, a friend of Gandhi's, back in 1935. Nonetheless, his outlook towards India and its people can hardly be described as progressive. For instance, in 1943, while his attentions were focused on the various crucibles of the world war, he did little to assist the Indian authorities in coping with a famine that wreaked havoc in Bengal, killing some 3 million people. It is true that he faced plenty enough problems closer to home, but the British government's unwillingness to divert any supplies to the subcontinent (which was, let it not be forgotten, providing huge numbers of troops to fight in Europe and North Africa) brought little credit to either the British authorities in general or Churchill individually.

Nor did his attitude to Gandhi cover him in much glory. According to Duff Cooper, Churchill's long-time political ally, in 1920 Churchill reacted to Gandhi's campaign of peaceful resistance by stating that he 'ought to be laid, bound hand and foot, at the gates of Delhi and then trampled on by an enormous elephant with the new Viceroy seated on its back'. In 1931 he condemned him as 'a seditious Middle Temple lawyer, now posing as a fakir of a type well known in the east'.

Somehow, these two grand men came to an accommodation, with Gandhi even claiming that he felt he could rely on Churchill's sympathy and goodwill. Certainly, Churchill came to realize that he could not hold back the tide of history. However, his desire to prolong the great British imperial saga for as long as possible often outstripped his concern for the interests of its imperial subjects. 'I hate Indians,' he said in 1942 after hearing the Indian Congress Party announce there would only be passive resistance to a Japanese invasion. It was a comment he intended to be taken ironically, but it nonetheless hinted at the ever-present tensions that existed between the ruler and the ruled.

# Make Time for Life's Finer Things

'I need a little more to drink. You see, I have a war to fight and I need fortitude for the battle.'

WINSTON CHURCHILL TO A
WHITE HOUSE BUTLER, 1943

There is a story that dates from Churchill's 1931 stay at New York's Plaza Hotel. Reception rang through to see if there was anything their esteemed guest wanted and Churchill, pretending to be his valet, told them: 'Mr Churchill is a man of simple tastes; he is quite easily satisfied with the best of everything.' There's many a true word spoken in jest, for Churchill truly did love the good life and would brook little compromise when it came to eating, drinking and smoking.

Food was never merely fuel for him, but a crucial part of life that ought to be relished. He had a formidable appetite from a young age, once receiving a thrashing at school for stealing sugar from a pantry. When on active service during the First World War, he sent a request to Clemmie for, among other things, corned beef, steak pie and Stilton. Stilton was his favourite cheese, although he could put up with Roquefort and Gruyère if the situation demanded. 'Stilton and port are like man and wife,' he once proclaimed. 'They should never be separated. "Whom God has joined together, let no man put asunder." No – nor woman either.'

**EAT LIKE CHURCHILL**

While Winston adored rich food, he generally liked plain cooking. Meat would ideally not be slathered in sauce, while soups were preferred clear or *petite marmite*. He enjoyed fish and seafood, plovers' eggs, beef, lamb and Yorkshire pudding, and to satisfy his sweet tooth there was little to rival a chocolate eclair. Curiously, he was insistent that breakfast should always be taken in bed and on one's own.

Despite Downing Street and the prime minister's country retreat, Chequers, theoretically eating off the ration book during the war, Churchill continued to dine well. In fact, a little too well. As his years advanced, so too did his expanding waistline. In the year before he died, Clemmie insisted he go on a diet. His response was to invest in a pair of scales that recorded his weight as lighter than the ones they'd previously employed. On being presented with a salad one evening, he argued: 'I have no grievance against the tomato but I believe one should eat other things as well.'

If Churchill's food intake caused angst, his voracious appetite for alcohol was an equally pressing concern. His opponents certainly raised it as an issue in the 1930s, so much so that President Roosevelt was doubtful about his suitability for the premiership. (Churchill, in turn, regarded America's prohibition experiment as a gross affront to personal freedom.) Yet for all his reputation as a drinker, there are scant instances of him ever being seen in public in a state of intoxication. Bessie Braddock may have had her suspicions and there was an episode at the 1943 Tehran Conference when some vodka served up by the Russian contingent got the better of him, but Churchill had few problems in holding his drink.

---

### DRINK LIKE CHURCHILL

Churchill developed a love for whisky while a young soldier in India. He did not like the taste at first but persevered so as not to have to drink so much of the local tea or water. It began a lifelong affair in which he was rarely to be found without a whisky and soda to hand. His favourite brand was Johnnie Walker, with both Red and Black labels acceptable. He also enjoyed a little port, brandy (Hine for preference) and Pol Roger Champagne. In fact, he once told Mme Odette Pol-Roger: 'I could not live without champagne. In victory, I deserve it.
In defeat, I need it.'

---

As the years passed, he enjoyed playing up to his reputation as a drinker. In 1952, for instance, he revealed to George VI that when he was young he made it a rule never to take a strong drink before lunch, but had since changed the terms to before breakfast. It was true enough that he started imbibing early and carried on through the day; however, contrary to popular belief, his drinks were generally heavily diluted with water. Even as Churchill encouraged the perception that he was always quaffing, he was actually a rather sensible drinker. Hence the line he was known to roll out on several occasions: 'All I can say is that I have taken more out of alcohol than alcohol has taken out of me.'

Then, of course, there was his taste for cigars. In 1999, the magazine *Cigar Aficionado* rated him their number-one cigar smoker of the twentieth century. Although he came to regret the vast quantity of money he spent on tobacco, he showed little inclination ever to scrimp on his habit. He once told his son Randolph that, given a choice of two cigars, 'pick the longest and the strongest'. His taste in high-grade cigars was consolidated by his trip to Cuba in 1895 and his favourite brand was *Romeo y Julieta*, although he also smoked *Camacho*.

He was unrepentant about the health implications. When required to travel by aeroplane during the Second World War, he even had his oxygen mask adapted so that he might be able to smoke through it. Working his way through about ten cigars a day, he tended to chew rather than inhale and often left them half-finished. In 1952, *The New York Times* reported an exchange he had with Field Marshal Montgomery, hero of El Alamein. 'I neither drink nor smoke and I am one hundred per cent fit,' said Monty, to which

Churchill responded: 'I drink and smoke and I am two hundred per cent fit.'

He even went as far as to suggest that cigars had kept him on the straight and narrow. In a 1931 article for the *Strand*, he wrote:

> How can I tell that the soothing influence of tobacco upon my nervous system may not have enabled me to comport myself with calm and with courtesy in some awkward personal encounter or negotiation, or carried me serenely through some critical hours of anxious waiting?

# Be Magnanimous
in Victory

'Nothing is more costly, nothing is
more sterile, than vengeance.'

WINSTON CHURCHILL, 1946

Churchill was once invited to come up with an inscription for a war memorial. His (unused) effort was: 'In war, Resolution. In defeat, Defiance. In victory, Magnanimity. In peace, Goodwill.' They are words that capture the essence of his attitude to conflict and peace. Key is the idea of magnanimity, the quality of being generous in victory.

This generosity of spirit towards a vanquished opponent may be seen in microcosm in the way he paid tribute to Neville Chamberlain, who died mere months after Churchill succeeded him as prime minister. Chamberlain had been Churchill's unrivalled domestic bête noire for a period in the 1930s. Churchill said of him in 1938: 'In the depths of that dusty soul there is nothing but abject surrender.' It was a crushing rebuke. Yet, responding to his death in November 1940, he was much more charitable in his choice of words: 'Whatever else history may or may not say about these terrible, tremendous years, we can be sure that Neville Chamberlain acted with perfect sincerity according to his lights and strove to the utmost of his capacity and authority, which were powerful, to save the world from the awful, devastating struggle in which we are now engaged …' Churchill understood there were times when one was best served by being merciful in one's treatment of opponents.

Despite his reputation among some as a warmonger, it was an attitude he extended to his enemies in war. Writing about a prospective peace deal with the Boers in 1900, he cautioned against being too harsh. 'Revenge may be sweet,' he wrote, 'but it is also most expensive.' He picked up the theme again in 1930's *My Early Life*: 'I have always urged fighting wars and other contentions with might and main till overwhelming victory, and then offering the hand of friendship to the vanquished.'

'The problems of victory are more agreeable than those of defeat, but they are no less difficult.'

WINSTON CHURCHILL, LATE 1942

By the time he was prime minister and seriously contemplating the defeat of the despised Nazis, he continued to urge circumspection. He knew hammering out a peace settlement would be a tricky proposition, but he also had a long enough memory to recall the damage done by the harsh terms of the Versailles Treaty that concluded the previous world war. Indeed, he was among those who wondered whether a more accommodating peace might have seen off Hitler's chances of ever gaining power.

When in 1944 there were noises from the US administration that Germany should be deprived of her industry in a post-war settlement and left to become a pastoral nation, Churchill spoke out quickly. 'I'm all for disarming Germany, but we ought not to prevent her living decently ... You cannot indict a whole nation,' he argued. At the Yalta Conference the following year, he continued his crusade against overly punitive reparations: 'If you want your horse to pull your wagon, you have to give him some hay.'

It was his contention that Europe's best hopes of a lasting peace lay with a 'spiritually great France and a spiritually great Germany'. His faith in magnanimity as a policy was rooted in deep pragmatism: kicking your enemy when he had conceded defeat would only make him more aggressive when he started to recuperate a little. The long-term interests of everyone, he was convinced, were best served by a world order in which all the great nations had a fair share of the pie. In a parliamentary debate on the United Nations in May 1944, he proclaimed: 'There must be room in this new great structure of the world for the happiness and prosperity of all and in the end it must be capable of bringing happiness and prosperity even to the guilty and vanquished nations.'

This open-handed approach to the enemy only stretched so far, though. When it came to individuals guilty of perpetrating war crimes, he was much less forgiving. He did not see eye to eye with those who lobbied for due judicial process to be observed for Hitler's henchmen at the Nuremberg Trials. In September 1944, for example, he demanded: 'Kill the criminals, but don't carry on the business for years.'

By April the following year, he was no keener on the trials that America wanted to establish, suggesting in a private note that they would be a 'farce'. 'All sorts of complications ensue as soon as you admit a fair trial,' he explained. 'I would take no responsibility for a trial – even though the US wants to do it. Execute the principal criminals as outlaws – if no ally wants them.' There was a touch of 'There but for the grace of God ...' to his argument too. Reflecting on the outcome of the trials to General Ismay in 1946, he somewhat wryly observed: 'It shows that if you get into a war, it is supremely important to win it. You and I would be in a pretty pickle if we had lost.'

Yet for all the pragmatism, to the very end of his career Churchill truly believed in his creed of magnanimity. Consider his words to the members of the House of Commons in 1952:

What is a prisoner of war? He is a man who has tried to kill you and, having failed to kill you, asks you not to kill him. Long before the Christian revelation, the world had found out by practice that mercy towards a beaten enemy was well worthwhile and that it was much easier to gain control over wide areas by taking prisoners than by making everyone fight to the death against you.

# Get the Churchill Look

'The coat was too long and too heavy as a morning coat and too short and skimpy as a frock. It gave the wearer a sort of glorified coachman appearance.'

**THE *TAILOR AND CUTTER*'S OPINION OF CHURCHILL'S WEDDING OUTFIT, 1908**

He may not have set pulses racing across the catwalks of the world's fashion capitals but Winston Churchill did have a look that made him instantly recognizable across the globe. Even today the silhouette of a homburg hat and a fat cigar serve as a sort of graphic shorthand for the man. Churchill was not about the high fashion. For him it was all about promoting his personal brand.

It was never likely that he would be a man who could trade on his good looks alone. Hovering somewhere between five foot seven and five foot eight, he was sportily robust in his youth but distinctly corpulent in later life. His complexion was pale, he had freckles and as a younger man boasted a head of reddish-brown hair that had earned him the nickname 'Copperknob' at school. Even the 'Wanted' poster issued after his escape from Pretoria in 1899 could only muster the word 'unassuming' to describe his overall look.

Yet, even if the raw materials were somewhat limited, Churchill learned how to style himself for maximum visual impact. He was, for one thing, a great wearer of hats. In 1934, the British Hat Council ran a campaign with the famous line: 'If you want to get ahead, get a hat.' Churchill could have been their poster boy. He had a vast collection of headgear and was regularly seen sporting a bowler, a homburg or a top hat.

He also liked to step out in suitable military garb (including headwear) when the occasion demanded. Some of these he was perfectly qualified to wear, such as his old corporal's uniform from his time with the 4th Hussars. Others, though, were chosen chiefly for the sake of appearances. For instance, as First Lord of the Admiralty he would sometimes wear the uniform of the Royal Yacht Squadron, despite having no first-hand naval heritage of his own.

His taste in civilian clothing was guided by his love of comfort. Prone to sensitive skin, he often wore decadent pure silk underwear. His suits, meanwhile, were made by some of the most eminent tailors in the land. His favourite was Henry Poole & Co. of Savile Row, who provided him with numerous fine-fitting suits, often adorned with chalk stripes. The look was usually finished off with a bow tie. A navy one with polka dots was his customary choice, so much so that the design today is known as the Blenheim in reference to its most famous wearer's birthplace.

But perhaps Churchill's greatest contribution to fashion was the creation of what became known as the 'siren suit'. So called because of its suitability in the event of an air raid, it was essentially an all-in-one outfit somewhere between the notorious modern-day 'onesie' and a boiler suit. His own children rather disparagingly referred to them as 'rompers'. Typically fastened by a combination of zips and buttons, the siren suit had large pockets and was designed with both comfort and practicality in mind.

They were made from a variety of materials, including wool and canvas, but Churchill took things a step further than most. He commissioned the tailors Turnbull & Asser to make him a selection of differently coloured velvet versions (examples of which may be seen today at his family home at Blenheim). Although the siren suit became synonymous with Churchill during the war, it is believed he came up with the basic design pre-war so that he might have something appropriate to wear while working on the grounds around Chartwell.

Then there were those times when he preferred to dispense with clothes altogether. For evidence of his love of the au naturel state, one need only recall the numerous tales from secretaries taking dictation while he was 'in the altogether'. And if their word is not sufficient, there is the notorious nude encounter with President Roosevelt (see 'Maintain a Sense of Humour'), an incident that prompted Churchill to tell King George VI: 'Sir, I believe I am the only man in the world to have received the head of a nation naked.'

# Maintain a Life Outside of Politics

'A man can wear out a particular part of his mind by continually using it and tiring it, just in the same way as he can wear out the elbows of his coat … to be really happy and really safe, one ought to have at least two or three hobbies, and they must all be real.'

WINSTON CHURCHILL, *PALL MALL*, 1925

While Churchill's was a life played out in great part in public, he strove to maintain a distinct private life, too. Although he could not keep himself away from politics for very long, he nonetheless boasted a prodigious list of other interests, to many of which he devoted significant time and attention.

He was a keen fan of music, with a particular taste for military marches and classics from the music hall. Stars such as Marie Lloyd and Harry Lauder provided him with endless aural delight, their innuendo-strewn songs appealing to his rather naughty sense of humour. He was also something of a devotee of the light operatic works of Gilbert and Sullivan, and counted Noël Coward among his personal circle. Indeed, he once fell into dispute with President Roosevelt at a dinner party over the precise lyrical content of Coward's 'Mad Dogs and Englishmen'.

Cinema was another passion, with the works of the Marx Brothers and Walt Disney finding particular approval. He was also a big fan of the English-born Hollywood star, Leslie Howard, and was reportedly very upset on hearing the news in 1943 that Howard was dead after the aeroplane he was travelling in was shot down by a German fighter.

---

**FILM BUFF**

*Lady Hamilton* (1941) was Churchill's all-time favourite film, and was a saga about the relationship between Lord Nelson and Lady Hamilton. Starring the real-life couple Laurence Olivier and Vivien Leigh, its plot had as a backdrop the tyranny of Napoleonic Europe. Some have argued that Churchill hoped that this particular theme would resonate with US audiences, increasing pressure on the White House to enter the Second World War. Whether it contributed anything to that goal is somewhat academic; Churchill adored the movie regardless and claimed to have watched it over eighty times.

---

Although rather too fond of fine food and drink to become an elite sportsman, he was nonetheless highly competent in several disciplines. He was a champion fencer, but it was horsemanship that most captured his imagination. He was a keen polo player, learning the game as a boy from an aristocratic background and honing his skills as a military man in India. He continued to play to a decent standard until he was into his fifties.

He was a keen hunter too, riding out with hounds even in his seventies, as well as enjoying big game hunting.

He was, by all accounts, a fine shot. Reflecting on a rhino hunt in his 1908 work, *My African Journey*, he hinted at some moral qualms: '… we it is who have forced the conflict by an unprovoked assault with murderous intent upon a peaceful herbivore … if there is such a thing as right and wrong between man and beast – and who shall say there is not? – right is plainly on his side …' But, as might be expected of someone of his social background in that era, he was able to put aside any queasiness he might have had. His love of horses, meanwhile, found a new outlet in the post-war era when he was persuaded to turn his mind to horseracing. Churchill eventually owned numerous animals, several of whom recorded successes on the track, most notably Colonist II.

He was a fan of several more sedentary pastimes too, some of which he described in an article on hobbies for *Pall Mall* in 1925. As a boy he had an interest in stamp collecting and card games (bezique was a particular favourite) and suggested that 'joinery, chemistry and bookbinding' all offered their own pleasures. He adored landscaping and especially, somewhat unexpectedly, bricklaying, to the extent that he became a member of the Guild of Bricklayers. He discussed this particular passion in Volume I of *The Second World War*:

I lived mainly at Chartwell, where I had much to amuse me. I built with my own hands a large part of two cottages and extensive kitchen-garden walls, and made all kinds of rockeries and waterworks and a large swimming pool which was filtered to limpidity and could be heated to supplement our fickle sunshine.

In short, he was a man who understood the value of filling your life with a variety of interests. He was particularly glad of them in those phases when his political career faltered, as in the 1930s. In fact, in that decade he was able to devote serious attention to the pastime that most engrossed him: painting.

## CHURCHILL THE PAINTER

'If Churchill were a painter by profession, he'd have no trouble making a living.'

PABLO PICASSO

Of all the many hobbies and pastimes in which Churchill dabbled, painting stood clear of the others for the unreserved pleasure it gave him. Yet it was not until 1915 in the aftermath of the Gallipoli calamity, when he was into his forties, that he took up his paintbrush with any real intent. At a time when Clemmie truly feared for her husband as he fought his demons and contemplated the apparent collapse of his political career, a relative was able to persuade him to try his hand at oil painting. As he would later reflect: '... the muse of painting came to my rescue.'

For the rest of his life, painting served as a kind of therapy. It was one of the very few activities that he did in absolute silence, providing him with total distraction from the worries of the world. In 1945, for instance, he eased himself through the bitter disappointment of losing the post-war general election by taking himself off to Italy's Lake Como for a painting holiday. How he used his art as an emotional release can be traced through the nature of his works. When he began, he seemed to be experimenting with a kind of dark expressionism, exemplified by a melancholy self-portrait he produced that set his sad-looking figure against a dark background. However, as time passed he settled on a style characterized by vibrant colours. The canvas, he came to understand, was a place to escape his darker thoughts, not to confront them. Perhaps unsurprisingly, then, Churchill was a particular fan of the French Impressionists.

Over the course of his painting career, he produced some 500 works. Most were done either at his home at Chartwell or on his travels. He would regularly insist that all his unwieldy artist's paraphernalia – including stools, easels, canvases and paint boxes – joined him on his exotic jaunts. Although he stated his belief that art should both look to the traditions of the past and embrace the innovations of the present, in truth he became a reasonably conservative exponent. He produced countless attractive, idealized landscapes, many of which were later reproduced on greetings cards. Those early dalliances with dark expressionism gave way to a decidedly middle-brow, easy-on-the-eye approach.

But as Picasso's observation on page 172 shows, he was by no means an artistic slouch, even if he turned his back on the avant-garde. Sir John Lavery, another respected painter, and an official artist of the First World War, said, 'Had he chosen painting instead of statesmanship, I believe he would have been a great master with the brush.'

Anglo-French post-Impressionist Paul Maze was one who deeply influenced Churchill, the two having met on the Western Front in the First World War. Churchill also received tips from Walter Sickert, the famous Camden Town Group painter who also happened to be an old family friend of Clementine's.

There was other recognition, too. In 1947, he had two works accepted by the Royal Academy, which he had submitted under the pseudonym David Winter. By the time he died, Churchill had exhibited no less than fifty of his works at the Academy. There would also be an international touring exhibition that took in the USA, Australia and New Zealand, attracting record numbers of visitors along the way.

During the Second World War, he produced just one completed canvas – a view over Marrakesh that speaks of tranquillity and, perhaps more pertinently, peacefulness. There were few greater honours he would bestow on friends than to give them one of his pieces. Had he devoted all his energies to his painting rather than to politics, he may well have made a serious mark on the art world. As it stands, he is acknowledged as a talented and capable enthusiast.

But Churchill was never in it for glory or acclaim. For him, it was all about personal satisfaction. In 1948 he published a volume entitled *Painting as a Pastime*, which was in fact two essays he had written for the *Strand Magazine* back in 1921/2, collected together for the first time. In this work he wrote of how he was less concerned with the production of a masterpiece than with what he described as the 'joyride in a paint box' he experienced.

Critically, painting also provided him with an outlet that allowed him to address his personal and political challenges with renewed vigour. He summed up his love of art in the following terms: 'Happy are the painters for they shall not be lonely. Light and colour, peace and hope will keep them company to the end, or almost to the end, of the day.' Indeed, he would ultimately declare that after his death he would like to spend his first million years in heaven devoted to painting so that he might eventually be able to master the skill.

# Carve Out a Legacy: the Search for a Lasting Peace

'What is the use of living, if it be not to strive for noble causes and to make this muddled world a better place for those who will live in it after we are gone?'

WINSTON CHURCHILL IN A
SPEECH IN SCOTLAND, 1908

By the time the Second World War had drawn to a conclusion, Churchill was by no means a young man. His had been a remarkable and turbulent career before 1939 and he emerged from the war a national hero. Long gone was the callow youth who pursued the fame and personal glory that his ego at some level demanded. Glory was his for ever, but the older Churchill was more interested in taking a broader and longer view of the world. As he told a meeting in Brussels a few months after the end of the conflict in 1945: 'The future stands before us to make or mar.'

His great desire now was to establish an international system that treated everyone fairly and offered the prospect of a lasting peace. Having been at the sharp end of two world wars, he was determined there should not be a third. It was an ambition he outlined in a speech in October 1951:

If I remain in public life at this juncture it is because, rightly or wrongly, but sincerely, I believe that I may be able to make an important contribution to the prevention of a Third World War and to bringing nearer that lasting peace settlement which the masses of the people of every race and in every land fervently desire.

Churchill had long been an advocate of 'collective security' – that is to say, an international system in which nations with broadly common interests bound their fates together so as to ward off the prospect of conflict and increase the individual safety of each. In 1938 he gave a speech in the House of Commons on the subject:

What is there ridiculous about collective security? The only thing that is ridiculous about it is that we have not got it. Let us see whether we cannot do something to procure a strong element of collective security for ourselves and for others.

Having seen off the Nazi menace, he was quite clear where the next fault lines lay: in the ideological conflict between the capitalist West and the communist East. Despite Russia having been a wartime ally, he had long loathed the rise of Bolshevism. For Churchill, Soviet communism was on a par with Hitler's Nazism. He said they reminded him of the North and South Poles: 'They are at opposite ends of the earth, but if you woke up at either Pole tomorrow morning you could not tell which one it was.'

In 1919 he had described Bolshevism as 'a great evil', a 'disease' and a 'pestilence'. 'My hatred of Bolshevism and Bolsheviks is not founded on their silly system of economics,' he told the House of Commons a year later, 'or their absurd doctrine of an impossible equality. It arises from the bloody and devastating terrorism which they practise in every land into which they have broken ...' A further twelve months on he attacked Russia's communists for driving 'man from the civilization of the twentieth century into a condition of barbarism worse than the Stone Age'.

Yet while Churchill was quick to see through Hitler and Mussolini, he was more ambivalent about Stalin. 'He is a man of massive outstanding personality,' he told Parliament in 1942, continuing, 'A man of inexhaustable courage and willpower ... a man with that saving sense of humour ... a deep, cool wisdom and a complete absence of illusions of any kind.' However, by no means was he blind to the difficulties of negotiating with him and the Moscow establishment. Three years earlier, for instance, he had memorably described Russia as 'a riddle wrapped in a mystery inside an enigma'. In 1944, he said:

Trying to maintain good relations with a communist is like wooing a crocodile. You do not know whether to tickle it under the chin or to beat it over the head. When it opens its mouth you cannot tell whether it is trying to smile or preparing to eat you up!

Nonetheless, he knew that the Allies would not have triumphed without the efforts and enormous sacrifices of the Soviet Union. Even in 1945 he felt there was a chance of reaching an acceptable agreement with Stalin on the post-war balance of power. That, of course, proved to be a vain hope. Churchill abhorred Stalin's rule in the USSR and, as his 'Iron Curtain' speech showed, realized it presented the greatest threat to world peace in the post-war age. 'Tyranny presents itself in various forms,' he said in a speech in Amsterdam in 1948, 'but it is always the same, whatever slogans it utters, whatever name it calls itself by, whatever liveries it wears. It is always the same and makes a demand on all free men to risk and do all in their power to withstand it.'

It was with this in mind that Churchill's later years of public life were devoted to a genuinely selfless quest for a politically balanced international system that could sustain lasting peace.

## CHURCHILL AND THE BOMB

'Another great war, especially an ideological war, fought as it would be not only on frontiers but in the heart of every land with weapons far more destructive than men have yet wielded, would spell the doom, perhaps for many centuries, of such civilization as we have been able to erect.'

WINSTON CHURCHILL IN A SPEECH IN
THE HOUSE OF COMMONS, 1944

As discussed earlier (see 'See Which Way the Wind is Blowing'), Churchill had been fearful since the 1920s of the development of atomic weapons. However, little could he have known then that he would play an instrumental role in the bomb's first deployment. As he told the House of Commons in August 1945 in the aftermath of the attacks by the USA on the Japanese cities of Hiroshima and Nagasaki: 'The decision to use the atomic bomb was taken by President Truman and myself at Potsdam, and we approved the military plans to unchain the dread, pent-up forces …'

It was an action he was keen to defend, arguing that had Germany or Japan developed the bomb first, they would not have held back from using it. 'Future generations will judge these dire decisions,' he said, 'and I believe that if they find themselves dwelling in a happier world from which war has been banished, and where freedom reigns, they will not condemn those who struggled for their benefit amid the horrors and miseries of this gruesome and ferocious epoch.'

The genie, he understood only too well, was out of the bottle. The world was divided ideologically and now had technology capable of unleashing hitherto unthinkable destruction. It was a subject that troubled him even as he came to the end of his road as a public servant. In his last address to Parliament, in March 1955, he observed ruefully:

We live in a period, happily unique in human history, when the whole world is divided intellectually and to a large extent geographically between the creeds of communist discipline and individual freedom, and when, at the same time, this mental and psychological division is accompanied by the possession by both sides of the obliterating weapons of the nuclear age.

The only workable strategy to secure peace, he concluded, was via the nuclear deterrent. The threat of mutual annihilation was, he was sure, the best hope of averting another major war. 'The day may dawn,' he concluded poignantly, 'when fair play, love for one's fellow men, respect for justice and freedom, will enable tormented generations to march forth serene and triumphant from the hideous epoch in which we have to dwell. Meanwhile, never flinch, never weary, never despair.'

The nuclear deterrent was a cause he had been championing for some years by then. It had quickly become apparent that Stalin was not the negotiating partner Churchill had hoped he might be. 'I tell you, it is no use arguing with a communist,' he had told an audience at New York's Ritz-Carlton Hotel in 1949. 'It's no good trying to convert a communist, or persuade him. You can only deal with them on the following basis … by having superior force on your side on the matter in question …'

While he faced a significant lobby campaigning for nuclear disarmament, it was an idea he could not stomach. As he put it to his fellow parliamentarians in 1950:

> The argument is now put forward that we must never use the atomic bomb until, or unless, it has been used against us first. In other words, you must never fire until you have been shot dead. That seems to me undoubtedly a silly thing to say and a still more imprudent position to adopt. Moreover, such a resolve would certainly bring war nearer.

He was by no means unsympathetic to those who found it 'melancholy' that peace between nations had 'no nobler foundation than mutual terror', but it was his opinion that there was no room for naïve idealism in the nuclear age. Instead, the world's leaders needed to find a practical solution to guarantee peace. However counter-intuitive it seemed, he was convinced that the bomb offered the best chance of achieving that goal.

In early 1952 he was in Washington, DC and he outlined his argument to Congress. 'It is my belief,' he said, 'that by accumulating deterrents of all kinds against aggression we shall, in fact, ward off the fearful catastrophe, the fears of which darken the life and mar the progress of all the peoples of the globe.' History would suggest that, for now at least, he has been proved right.

# Think Global

'It is no exaggeration to say that the future of
the whole world and the hopes of a broadening
civilization founded upon Christian ethics depend
upon the relations between the British Empire or
Commonwealth of Nations and the USA.'

WINSTON CHURCHILL, ANNOUNCING LORD HALIFAX
AS THE NEW AMBASSADOR TO THE U.S., 1941

As a man brought up on empire, Churchill had always been outward-looking. Domestic politics fascinated him but the global landscape utterly gripped him. In his pursuit of a happy post-war global balance, he became increasingly convinced that Britain needed to bind herself tightly to her cousins across the Atlantic Ocean. Little old Britain may have gamely stood alone against Hitler's Germany for a while, but Churchill realized that the country was in no state to go it alone in the long-term.

Although he longed for the preservation of Britain and its empire, he acknowledged that the international situation had changed over his lifetime, and not greatly to Britain's advantage. In 1928 he warned his fellow MPs: '… this new twentieth century is not in many ways so favourable to us as the nineteenth century. A new world is growing up around us, far larger than anything previously seen, and filled with giant states and competitors.'

There was serious doubt whether the country would be able to endure another major war, having emerged from the two world wars unbroken but distinctly weakened. If his ambition of 'collective security' was to work, Britain must ally herself with powerful friends. And since it was evident that the superpowers of the post–war age were the USA and the USSR, it was natural that London should turn towards Washington.

## A SPECIAL RELATIONSHIP

Churchill, of course, had a natural affinity with the States, being half-American on his mother's side. He made his first visit to the country in 1895 and was immediately enamoured, calling the Americans an extraordinary people. He also marvelled at their hospitality and how they made him feel more at home and at ease than even in Britain. Indeed, many of his British contemporaries thought Churchill displayed some traits of an American, most notably his propensity for showmanship. However, it was partly his love of employing flowery speech and his effusive praise for America that played a large part in the US's providing vital aid to Britain during the war, setting the scene for any future relationship.

His desire for closer union between the two nations was there from the outset: the key union of the 'English–

speaking peoples' as he saw it. In 1918, he told a meeting of Americans in London:

Deep in the hearts of the people of these islands … lay the desire to be truly reconciled before all men and all history with their kindred across the Atlantic Ocean, to blot out the reproaches and redeem the blunders of a bygone age … to create once more a union of hearts, to write once more a history in common.

He would expound a similar message for the rest of his life. For instance, on Boxing Day 1941 he told the US Congress:

It is not given to us to peer into the mysteries of the future. Still, I avow my hope and faith, sure and inviolate, that in the days to come the British and American peoples will for their own safety and for the good of all walk together side by side in majesty, in justice and in peace.

Then in a speech delivered at Harvard University two years later, he suggested the US had a moral responsibility to put itself at the centre of the international stage:

The price of greatness is responsibility. If the people of the United States had continued in a mediocre station, struggling with the wilderness, absorbed in their own affairs, and a factor of no consequence in the movement of the world, they might have remained forgotten and undisturbed beyond their protecting oceans: but one cannot rise to be in many ways the leading community in the civilized world without being involved in its problems, without being convulsed by its agonies and inspired by its causes.

Fast-forward seven years to an Independence Day speech he made in London:

The drawing together in fraternal association of the British and American peoples, and of all the peoples of the English-speaking world, may well be regarded as the best of the few good things that have happened to us and to the world in this century of tragedy and storm.

While it was clear, though rarely acknowledged by officialdom, that the UK was the junior partner in the new special relationship, Churchill characteristically refused to play up to the role too readily. In 1949, for instance, he told a gathering in New York: 'You may be larger and we may be older. You may be the stronger, sometimes we may be the wiser.' And in 1951 he explicitly stated: 'I have never accepted a position of subservience to the United States.'

Yet there could be no hiding from the fact that this was no marriage of equals. As the US prospered, Britain endured years of austerity while its erstwhile empire dissolved away. There were more obvious imbalances, too. America's refusal to assist Britain in developing the bomb in the post-war era and her refusal to support British actions during the 1956 Suez Crisis provide two of the starkest examples.

Much of this was difficult for a figure as proud as Churchill to swallow, but he did so in the interests of collective security. There was more at stake than mere national pride. He told Parliament in November 1950:

Here in Britain, and I doubt not throughout the British Empire and Commonwealth of Nations, we always follow a very simple rule, which has helped us in maintaining the safety of this country: 'The worse things get, the more we stand together.' Let it also be seen that the English-speaking world follows the same plan.

While he regarded the US–UK relationship as pivotal to Britain's long-term safety, it was but one element in a more complex international picture. Crucially, he called for what he famously described in 1946 as a 'kind of United States of Europe' from which 'no nation should be permanently outcast'. This, he argued, was the only way to ensure there was no repeat of the circumstances that had resulted in two devastating world wars. Europe, it can be argued, continues to struggle with exactly what form this union should take and Churchill himself was dubious about the direction of what by the end of his life was called the European Economic Community. Nonetheless, those countries who have come into the union have consistently striven to resolve their myriad difficulties by non-military means.

The third pillar in his vision of collective security was the creation of an effective United Nations to replace what had proved to be its toothless predecessor, the League of Nations. As early as 1938 he was advocating:

> If the League of Nations has been mishandled and broken, we must rebuild it. If a league of peace-seeking peoples is set at naught, we must convert it into a league of armed peoples, too faithful to molest others, too strong to be molested themselves.

Churchill had twice borne witness to catastrophe caused by a world of disunited states acting in their own interests. Post-1945, he recognized the new battle lines being drawn between East and West. He reckoned that peace might nonetheless reign via a three-pronged internationalist approach: a strong Anglo-American relationship, a united Europe (at least comprising its Western states) and a supranational body granted real power. It was, as history has shown, a plan beset with difficulties. Nonetheless, the world has indeed managed to avoid another world war thus far.

# Come to an Accommodation with God

'I am not a pillar of the Church but a buttress – I support it from outside.'

WINSTON CHURCHILL, AS RECALLED BY HIS PRIVATE SECRETARY, SIR ANTHONY MONTAGUE BROWNE

For a man born in the Victorian period and raised in a conventionally upper-class environment, Churchill's relationship with religion was notably complex. Someone of his background would typically have been expected to see the Church not only as a place of spirituality but also as a fundamental cornerstone on which the social order was built. Churchill clearly valued it in the latter sense, but his personal faith was uncertain and subject to change.

That said, it would be misleading to suggest that he was in any meaningful way anti-religious or anti-God. Instead, his association with organized religion was what might be termed malleable. He harboured an intellectual uncertainty about the nature of a divinity and the presence of an afterlife, but had a fundamental belief in the existence of an overriding guiding force in the universe. More pragmatically, he saw Christianity as providing a sound moral code by which society could, and indeed ought to, be governed.

No doubt the early death of his father seriously shook his faith. But having been versed in conventional

Christianity at his various schools, his first real religious crisis occurred when he went to India in 1896. While he was there he read Winwood Reade's 1872 work, *The Martyrdom of Man*. The Victorian prime minister, William Gladstone, had earlier condemned the book as 'irreligious' for its secular and social Darwinist approach to history, although Reade himself was not an atheist. The volume had quite an effect on Churchill, making him question his fundamental beliefs and leading him into a period of atheism.

Yet, influenced by his experiences on the battle lines, Churchill eventually came back to a trust in some sort of higher force. While he was unable to embrace the idea of a benevolent godhead of the sort he had been brought up on, he believed there was a unifying guiding spirit at play in the world. It might best be described in terms of an impersonal 'providence', with Churchill equally convinced that 'providence' had great things planned for him. His sense that destiny had taken him in its hands came through in a conversation he had in 1906 with Violet Asquith: 'We are all worms,' said Churchill, 'but I believe I am a glow-worm.'

His theological ideology was neatly summed up in an address he gave at Westminster Abbey at the unveiling of the Commando Memorial there on 21 May 1948: '… we have our faith that the universe is ruled by a supreme being and in fulfilment of a sublime moral purpose.' It was hardly the stuff of brimstone and fire, but reflected his desire to play it cool when it came to religion.

He attended church services only sporadically and was known to be critical of church politics, with bishops and archbishops often coming in for a particular scolding.

In the opinion of Geoffrey Fisher, the Archbishop of Canterbury from 1945 until 1961, Churchill believed in a god, but one mainly concerned with the well-being of Britain. This opinion was borne out by a motion Churchill put before the House of Commons on VE Day in 1945: 'That this House do now attend at the church of St Margaret, Westminster, to give humble and reverent thanks to Almighty God for our deliverance from the threat of German domination.'

Churchill's reflections on death and what might follow are also informative. As a young man he had been convinced he was destined for an early demise, just as his father had been (of course, this proved not to be the case, although the two shared the same date of passing, 24 January). Essentially, it seems that he believed that death represented a permanent ending, rather than a new beginning. In July 1953, as an old man aware that death may not be long in coming for him, he announced that he did 'not believe in another world; only in black velvet – eternal sleep'. Certainly the prospect of dying did not cow him, as his adventures as a young man that put him in death's way on more than one occasion show. 'When it comes to dying,' he was known to say, 'I will not complain, I will not miaow.'

But for all that, he was careful not to let his religious beliefs (or lack of them) interfere with his political life.

As many leaders have come to realize, politics and religion rarely mix well. He did understand, though, that much of the public at large were committed to traditional religious adherence (even if the atrocities of the First World War had seen many question their faith). So it is little surprise that his wartime speeches are littered with appeals to God. Furthermore, whatever his own reservations about the afterlife, he knew the concept offered solace to a people wearied by losing loved ones and living under the threat of violent death themselves. In a parliamentary speech on 8 September 1942, he said, 'Only faith in a life after death in a brighter world where dear ones will meet again – only that and the measured tramp of time can give consolation.'

In addition, he had a genuine belief in the worthiness of 'Christian ethics' and 'Christian civilization', phrases that crop up repeatedly in his speeches before, during and after the war. So, for instance, in June 1940 he advised the Commons: 'I expect that the Battle of Britain is about to begin. Upon this battle depends the survival of Christian civilization.' A little less than a year later, he told Harry Hopkins (one of President Roosevelt's closest advisers and also much admired by Churchill): 'We can find nothing better than Christian ethics on which to build, and the more closely we follow the Sermon on the Mount, the more likely we are to succeed in our endeavours.'

Churchill, then, seems to have embraced religion more for the social advantages it offered than in search of personal salvation. In truth, he mostly seems to have treated the idea of a personal god with some amusement. So it is reported in Walter Graebner's 1949 work, *My Dear Mr Churchill*: 'I wouldn't have His job for anything. Mine is hard enough, but His is much more difficult. And – umph – He can't even resign.' Also consider his ruminations shared with an audience on the occasion of his seventy-fifth birthday: 'I am ready to meet my Maker. Whether my Maker is prepared for the ordeal of meeting me is another matter.'

Wherever he was headed, following his death in 1965, over 300,000 people passed by his coffin to wish him well on his way as he lay in state in Westminster Hall.

# The Greatest Briton

'The journey has been enjoyable and
well worth making – once.'

PURPORTED WORDS OF WINSTON CHURCHILL
TO HIS SON-IN-LAW, CHRISTOPHER SOAMES,
FROM HIS DEATHBED, 1965

Via a combination of his own recklessness and some ill-fortune, Churchill had endured several brushes with the Grim Reaper but, perhaps against the odds, made it to his tenth decade. As reported in *London to Ladysmith Via Pretoria*, in 1899 he had told a Boer soldier who claimed he would fight for ever: 'Wait and see how you feel when the tide is running the other way. It does not seem so easy to die when death is near.' Yet there is the suspicion, as the quotation at the start of this section suggests, that Churchill was ready to go. Beset by long-term ill health, he had become increasingly withdrawn from the world around him. Sometime in early January 1965 he is said to have told Soames, who was proffering him a glass of his favourite champagne at the time: 'I'm so bored with it all.' For someone who had led such an action-packed life, the slow deterioration of his faculties must have been unbearably infuriating.

He died at his home in London on 24 January 1965 after suffering a stroke earlier in the month from which he never regained consciousness. At the end he was surrounded by his wife and children. At least one of his wishes had been fulfilled – when he broke a hip in Monte

Carlo two years earlier, he had been convinced the end was nigh and had pleaded: 'I want to die in England.'

It is the normal fate of the politician (and particularly those who achieve real power) to be irredeemably unpopular with a good part of the population, but news of Churchill's demise met with an extraordinary and virtually universal outpouring of grief. Of course, not everyone agreed with his politics. Even Churchill had ended up disagreeing with some of his choices. But few refused to acknowledge the unique contribution he had made to the fate of the nation. It was quite possible for even the biggest cynic to look past the faults he no doubt had and to recognize the great sacrifices he had made to guide his country through a terrible and debilitating war, at an age when he had believed his most successful days were behind him.

> 'We are a free people because a man
> called Winston Churchill lived.'
>
> THE *SPECTATOR* MAGAZINE, 1965

The response to his death tells us much about the man himself. He was, for one, the only civilian in the twentieth century to be granted a state funeral. Queen Elizabeth II's statement summed up the national mood:

I know that it will be the wish of all my people that the loss which we have sustained by the death of the Right Honourable Sir Winston Churchill, K.G., should be met in the most fitting manner, and that they should have an opportunity of expressing their sorrow at the loss and their veneration of the memory of that outstanding man who in war and peace served his country unfailingly for more than fifty years and in the hours of our greatest danger was the inspiring leader who strengthened and supported us all.

Thousands lined the streets of London to see his funeral procession go by, and millions more watched on television. Representatives from 112 countries packed St Paul's Cathedral for the funeral service itself. Afterwards, his body was transferred by train to Oxfordshire and he was buried in the churchyard at Bladon, close to Blenheim where he had entered the world ninety years before. In accordance with his wishes, the interment was a low-key affair, with only close family present. It was a pleasingly dignified conclusion to a life that had been played out so extensively in public.

Nor was the affection evident for Churchill restricted to the UK. Tributes came from around the world and his status as the greatest leader of the twentieth century was enshrined. The American publication *Time* had named him their 'Man of the Half-Century' in 1950, which gives an idea of the high esteem in which he was held internationally. By the end of the century, the same magazine had placed Einstein above him for their 'Man of the Century' accolade. There was plenty of debate about that decision, but it is telling that Churchill remained in contention. The argument broadly went that Einstein had redefined scientific knowledge but Churchill had defeated tyranny. Who can really say which achievement is the greater?

Churchill's enduring appeal was further illustrated when on 24 November 2002 he was named 'the greatest Briton of all time' in a national poll that attracted more than a million votes. He received some 60,000 votes more than his nearest rival for the title, the engineer Isambard Kingdom Brunel. Churchill would no doubt have dismissed such a contest as trivial. We might also suspect that deep down he would have loved to know the honour was his.

'National heroes are legion: much more rare are the great men whose action equally benefits the world and their country. If he belongs to Great Britain, Churchill also belongs to the world and in particular to the Western world.'

*LE DEVOIR* (MONTREAL NEWSPAPER), 1965

# Selected Bibliography

Best, Geoffrey, *Churchill: A Study in Greatness*, Penguin (2002)

Bonham-Carter, Violet, *Winston Churchill As I Knew Him*, Collins (1965)

Churchill, Randolph S. & Gilbert, Martin, *Winston S. Churchill*, Heinemann (1967-82)

Churchill, Winston, *A History of the English-Speaking Peoples*, Cassell (1956-58)

Churchill, Winston, *Lord Randolph Churchill*, Macmillan (1907)

Churchill, Winston, *Marlborough: His Life and Times*, Sphere (1967)

Churchill, Winston, *My Early Life: A Roving Commission*, Thornton Butterworth (1930)

Churchill, Winston, *Savrola*, Longman, Green & Co. (1900)

Churchill, Winston, *The Second World War*, Cassell (1948-54)

Churchill, Winston, *The Story of the Malakand Field Force 1897*, Longman, Green & Co. (1899)

# Selected Bibliography

Churchill, Winston, *The World Crisis*, Thornton Butterworth (1923–31)

Colville, John, *Footprints in Time: Memories*, Collins (1976)

Gilbert, Martin, *Churchill: A Life*, Pimlico (2000)

Gilbert, Martin, *Churchill: The Wilderness Years*, Macmillan (1981)

Graebner, Walter, *My Dear Mr Churchill*, Michael Joseph (1965)

hansard.millbanksystems.com

Jenkins, Roy, *Churchill: A Biography*, Pan (2002)

Kelly, Brian & Smyer, Ingrid, *The Best Little Stories of Winston Churchill*, Cumberland House Publishing (2008)

Langworth, Richard M. (ed.), *Churchill in His Own Words*, Ebury Press (2012)

Nel, Elizabeth, *Mr Churchill's Secretary*, Hodder & Stoughton (1958)

Rhodes James, Sir Robert, *Churchill: A Study in Failure, 1900-1939*, Weidenfeld & Nicolson (1970)

Singer, Barry, *Churchill Style: The Art of Being Winston Churchill*, Abrams Image (2012)

Soames, Mary, *Clementine Churchill*, Cassell (1979)

Taylor, A. J. P., *English History 1914-1945*, OUP (1965)

Toye, Richard, *Churchill's Empire: The World That Made Him and the World He Made*, Pan (2011)

Toye, Richard, *The Roar of the Lion: The Untold Story of Churchill's World War II Speeches*, OUP (2013)

www.winstonchurchill.org